VAINGLORY: THE FORGOTTEN VICE

VAINGLORY:

THE FORGOTTEN VICE

Rebecca Konyndyk DeYoung

WILLIAM B. EERDMANS PUBLISHING COMPANY
Grand Rapids, Michigan / Cambridge, U.K.

Published 2014 by

Wm. B. Eerdmans Publishing Co.

2140 Oak Industrial Drive n.e., Grand Rapids, Michigan 49505 /

P.O. Box 163, Cambridge cb3 9pu U.K.

www.eerdmans.com

Printed in the United States of America

19 18 17 16 15 14   7 6 5 4 3 2 1

Library of Congress Cataloging-in-Publication Data

DeYoung, Rebecca Konyndyk.

Vainglory: the forgotten vice / Rebecca Konyndyk DeYoung.

pages   cm

Includes bibliographical references and index.

ISBN 978-0-8028-7129-9 (pbk.: alk. paper)

1. Pride and vanity. 2. Deadly sins.   I. Title.

BV4627.P7D49   2014

241´.3 — dc23

2014031193

The author and publisher gratefully acknowledge permission to reprint Madeleine L'Engle's "People in Glass Houses" from *The Ordering of Love,* published by Waterbrook Press in 2005 and copyright © 2005 by Crosswicks, Ltd.

Unless otherwise noted, the Scripture quotations in this publication are from the HOLY BIBLE: NEW INTERNATIONAL VERSION. Copyright © 1973, 1978, 1984 by the International Bible Society. Used by permission of Zondervan Bible Publishers.

Contents

Acknowledgments

This book is the fruit of many conversations and wisdom gathered from many sources throughout history. If it does nothing but pass along the wisdom of others in ways that we can appropriate in fresh ways today, writing it will have been worthwhile. There are more people to thank for that wisdom than I can fit on a single page, but I would be remiss not to mention those that I can.

I would like to thank Calvin College and Seminary for inviting me to give the 2010 Stob Lectures, which I have expanded into this book. Questions and suggestions from audiences at those lectures and other talks have importantly shaped what I've written. I also received sabbatical funding from Calvin College, the Calvin Center for Christian Scholarship, and the Louisville Institute. This funding provided essential time to prepare the manuscript for publication. I am grateful to Gayle Boss for her meticulous work in helping me translate my academic prose into something more readable. Several colleagues and friends graciously took the time to read part or all of the manuscript at various stages, including Kevin Timpe, Mary VandenBerg, Lois Konyndyk, members of the Calvin College philosophy department, and my senior seminar students. I would also like to thank Jon Pott and Mary Hietbrink at Eerdmans for their editorial suggestions and their encouragement throughout the publication process.

Finally, I would like to thank the family and friends who have prayed for me and supported my work on this project. This book is dedicated to my husband, Scot, who models the sort of unselfconscious integrity that makes virtue winsome and vainglory easy to avoid.

Psalm 8

LORD, our Lord, how majestic is your name in all the earth!
You have set your glory above the heavens.

Through the praise of children and infants
you have established a stronghold against your enemies,
to silence the foe and the avenger.

When I consider your heavens, the work of your fingers,
the moon and the stars, which you have set in place,
what are mere mortals that you are mindful of them,
human beings that you care for them?

You have made them a little lower than the heavenly beings
and crowned them with glory and honor.
LORD, our Lord, how majestic is your name in all the earth!

Verses 1-5 and 9, TNIV

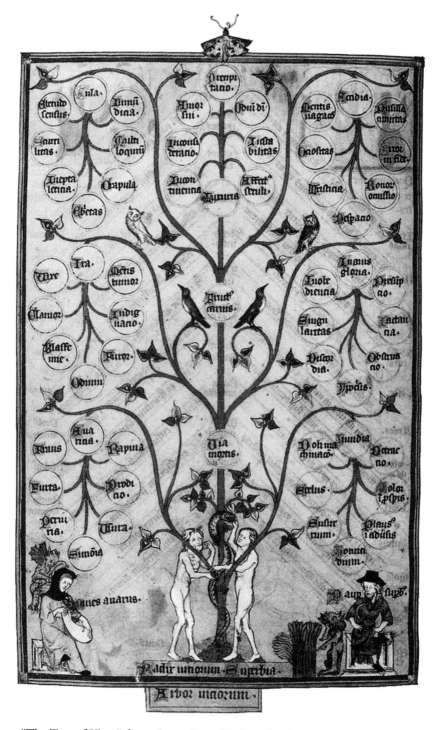

"The Tree of Vices" from the psalter of Robert de Lisle, fourteenth century.
Used with permission of the British Library.

Introduction

You're so vain, you probably think this song is about you.

Carly Simon, "You're So Vain"

IN OCTOBER 2010 I delivered much of the material in this book as the Stob Lectures at Calvin College. Talking about vainglory quickly turned out to be an awkward project — and not only because philosophers tend to be socially awkward people. It was also ethically awkward. Giving the talks meant I had to explain to my audience the ways in which the limelight and applause from other people bring certain spiritual risks. To do that, of course, I had to stand in front of my audience, right there in the limelight. I knew I could expect some applause at the end. How would I maintain any credibility if I lectured about how vainglory is a vice while vaingloriously enjoying the limelight and my audience's applause? On the other hand, if I *didn't* glory in their response to my lectures, how would my audience know that I was genuinely humble and not just putting on a false show of it? And what if I secretly hoped I'd get glory for *that?* Whether I acted from virtue or vice, the trap of vainglory could snare me either way. It was almost impossible not to be paralyzed by the temptations all around me!

As the date of the lectures drew nearer, I pondered what to do about this. I wanted to give genuinely interesting and worthwhile talks. I also wanted to make a good impression and maintain my academic reputation (such as it is). So my motives were truly mixed. Should I admit that? I wasn't particularly eager to put my own moral faults on display by publicly exhibiting the very vice I was supposed to be warning my audiences about: "See me? I'm exhibit A. Which is a great reason to take me seriously, since I can't practice what I preach." Or should I fake total purity? I was sure I couldn't pull that off, and I wasn't excited about exposing my dark hypocritical side to my audience, either. Unfortunately, I can often be very comfortable about the gap between my walk and my talk — as long as no one else gets to point it out to me in front of a very large audience.

I finally decided to handle my potential temptation by turning it to someone else's profit. I would offer my students who attended extra credit if they could catch me being vainglorious as I delivered the lectures. At the very least, I reasoned, it would be a useful diagnostic exercise for them! As someone once quipped, "If you can't be a good example, at least you can serve as a horrible warning." But of course, if the students gloried in their remarkable ability to spot my vainglorious actions, they would join me in falling victim to the same vice.

Here's the real irony: a series of lectures on vainglory could serve as a horrible warning about the ways you can go wrong *even when trying to be a good example.* It doesn't take too long to see how tricky this vice can be to avoid, does it? My predicament put me in good company, however. Christian preacher and church father Saint Augustine (354-430 A.D.) famously confesses his struggles with vainglory, too.[1] Only you can decide whether it is reputation-enhancing for me to compare myself to a saint — *when* he's committing and confessing his sins! If we all stand in danger of vainglory, however, our common task will be to figure out how to deal with this perennial human pitfall.

Masters of the Art of Fame

"Vainglory" may be an unfamiliar and archaic name for a vice, but the problem it names is familiar enough. And it's good to have a label for it, because the concept of vainglory is worth putting back in our conceptual toolbox. It's a temptation as pressing and relevant today as it ever was. And in this instance, that "ever" goes back a long, long way.

Vainglory was on the original list of the "deadly sins" — a list of vices first compiled over 1600 years ago. The list of seven has recently become familiar again. Twenty years ago, most Protestant college students couldn't name more than one or two of the deadly sins, if they had even heard of them at all. The only people who could rattle off all seven were

Catholic kids drilled in catechism class. Now there are all sorts of references to the seven deadly sins in popular culture. *Harper's* magazine did a terrifically funny spoof on the sins in 1987 in which Madison Avenue ad agencies were asked to create advertisements for each of the seven. (The ad on greed featured advice from Santa.) MTV did an hour-long special on the vices in 1993, interviewing people like Queen Latifah and Kirstie Alley, and the History Channel ran a series in 2010, complete with low-budget fire-and-brimstone sound effects. Thanks to the star power of Brad Pitt and Morgan Freeman in the hit movie *Se7en,* the seven deadlies have recaptivated the American popular imagination. Kansas State University researchers created a color-coded map of each state according to how sinful it was, and everything from Dr. Seuss to SpongeBob Squarepants characters have been analyzed by the vices they represent. A Google search on "seven deadly sins" turns up Web sites selling t-shirts, posters, and even color-coded wristbands, so that you can "flaunt your fatal flaws."[2] You'll also find articles about the seven deadly sins of home remodeling. There's even a Seven Deadly Sins board game which requires you to "sin to win." And if you do win, you can toast your victory with a bottle of wine called The Seven Deadly Zins (yes, a Zinfandel). The Web site for the wine offers you a drinking song and tips on how to commit gluttony too — by pairing your wine with delectable chocolate desserts.

If you read any of these contemporary lists of the seven deadly sins, however, you'll notice that they don't include vainglory. The list will read as it does on the DVD cover of *Se7en:* gluttony, greed, sloth, envy, wrath, pride, and lust. What happened to vainglory? Compounding this mystery is the fact that most people don't know off the top of their heads what vainglory is, how it is different from vanity or pride, who invented it and when, why it made the original list of deadly sins, and why it isn't on the list anymore. What's the story with vainglory?

If we want a glimpse of what vainglory is, pop culture supplies a host of characters. Take music star Lady Gaga. She's made such a splashy sensation in American culture that she's earned a spot on the cover of *Time* magazine's "Top 100 Most Influential People of 2010" issue. The title of her first album — *The Fame* — and many of her hit songs — "Starstruck" and "Applause" among them — are about being famous and followed after. On her third album, *Born This Way,* she invites her audience to join her in believing that "we are all born superstars." Lady Gaga's appearance and videos are expressly designed to shock and titillate her audiences and to draw attention to herself. Let's just say by way of summary that she's taken the Marilyn-Monroe-and-Madonna thing to a whole new level. As she reports, "I am a master of the art of fame."[3]

If this lady's glitz is a little too much for you, try watching a vain Disney character show off instead. In the 1991 Disney film *Beauty and the Beast,* Gaston sits glumly in the town tavern, rejected by heroine Belle. She wants a man of substance, not just show. His friends cheer him up by singing him a rousing song to remind him of how popular and well-liked he is by everyone else: "Every guy here'd love to be you, Gaston. . . ./ There's no man in town as admired as you./You're everyone's favorite guy./ Everyone's awed and inspired by you,/And it's not very hard to see why."

According to the rest of the song, Gaston is known for his prowess in expectorating, using antlers in all of his decorating, eating several dozen (raw) eggs for breakfast, and being covered with hair — every last inch of him. In fact, the lyrics of "Gaston's Song" include examples of every single form of vainglory identified by Thomas Aquinas in the *Summa theologiae.* (Somebody at Disney did their medieval history homework!) To illustrate Gaston's vainglory, Disney borrows the traditional trope of a person gazing at himself in a mirror. Gaston is, as everyone can see, a dazzling specimen of manliness. It takes a smart girl like Belle to see through all of it and turn instead to a Beast with an ugly appearance but a heart of gold.

Even better, we can become these vainglorious characters ourselves. Modeling agencies such as IMTA (the International Modeling and Talent Association) invite young men and women from ages as young as three to display a cosmetically enhanced and fashionable appearance for the world to ooh and aah over. And their parents can encourage them. One aspiring teen model reports her mother's advice: "Always shine, never blend."[4]

But, you might object, you're not famous, outrageous, or popular in your local tavern. You're not a celebrity or even a celebrity wanna-be. If only that were enough to get us off the hook.

It turns out that vainglory can be a vice for nerds, too. For example, Garrison Keillor confesses, "I lust after recognition. I am desperate to win all the little merit badges and trinkets of my profession, and I am of less real use in this world than any good cleaning lady."[5] At professional conferences, college professors love to ask questions that are not really questions but are rather mini-lectures complete with name-dropping and erudite vocabulary, delivered with appropriately furrowed brows, so that even though no one understands the questions, everyone comes away with an impression of how smart they are. "Scientific experts" and their white lab coats have their own version of this game. The American public tends to judge debating politicians more on the image they present to their audience than on the views they express. (Does this candidate look "properly presidential"?) We don't need Hollywood. We can pull off the same vainglorious stunts in class, in court, or at city hall.

Or on Facebook. This social network, too, is all about projecting a public image of ourselves to get others' attention. Is your life interesting enough to post three times a day? Are your kids cute enough to showcase there in a photo album? If not, can you tell us how much you enjoy your morning coffee with lots of exclamation points and emoticons anyway? To make you more interesting to read about, Facebook offers help: It can search for more friends for you if you don't already have enough. How often do other people check your page? How often do *you* check it? How flattering or goofy is your profile picture? How long did it take you to carefully choose it? How many friends post on your wall, and how often do they "like" your latest witty posting?

Last but not least, there is the matter of greatest concern to the Christian tradition. How many of us want to appear to others as good Christian people? And to what extent do we care more about *appearing* good to others than about actually *being* good? As a parent who takes four young children to church every Sunday, I usually herd my family to the balcony. It's not simply because I worry about distracting others from worship (although I am concerned about that, too). It's because I know I can't pull off that perfect-family-with-the-obedient-and-polite-well-behaved-children look in public.

It's not just my kids' behavior that has the potential to make me look bad. Many Sundays (and many weekdays, too), I would love be able to pull off even a convincing appearance of personal piety, but my hypocritical cover wears thin. And sometimes church can be the least forgiving place when it comes to having our flaws on display. So, like the Pharisees, we work extra hard to make sure other people can tell that we fit in the cate-

5

gory of Good, Upstanding, and Respectable People. Or perhaps we're not content to fly under the radar in our Christian walk; we'd like to be well-known and warmly appreciated as a community leader, a prayer warrior, or an engaging preacher. Jesus saw the temptation in this. In the Gospel of Matthew (6:1), he warns his disciples not to be like the Pharisees: "Be careful not to do your 'acts of righteousness' before [others], to be seen by them."[6]

The bottom line: Vainglory is a vice for all of us — as tempting now as it was in the fourth century. Love of fame may be the most obvious or extreme form of this vice, but the truth is, we can *all* be overly attached to how we appear to others and are acknowledged and approved by them. So philosophers like me can't get away with mocking celebrities, although that would be easier to write about and certainly a lot more fun. Vainglory is not just other people's problem; it is *our* problem. Vainglory is not a sin that specially plagues secular glory-seekers; it is, in an important way, a vice that plagues the Christian life. To paraphrase Carly Simon's famous 1972 song, whether you're Paris Hilton or a Pharisee, whether you're glorying in shallow, socially respectable appearances or spiritual virtues, "You're so vain, you probably think this book is about you." And you just may be right.

A Translation — *For* Transformation

This book is my attempt to return vainglory to the limelight, to expose this spiritual problem and see more clearly its subtle incursion into our hearts, whether in obvious or subtle ways. There's more to this project, however, than just making us all feel guilty. There's no point in pointing out our moral defects if we don't care, or if we do care but we don't know what to do about them. As N. T. Wright wryly put it, "Christians seem to me to divide into two groups nowadays: the first lot don't think that sin matters very much anyway, and the second know perfectly well that it does, but still can't kick the habit."[7]

In the tradition I'm working from, the reason to care about vice is that it keeps us from drawing closer to God (and other people) in love. That love relationship is what we are made for; it's the cause of our deepest happiness. If we care about that, we will also care about obstacles that damage that relationship and thereby hinder our happiness. The purpose of growing in love — rather than avoiding vice out of some disconnected sense of obligation or guilt — is the frame for everything else I say in this book. It's also important not to paralyze ourselves with an obsessive focus on vice and sin. As we'll see, many past thinkers who analyzed the vice of vainglory did so for medicinal purposes. Like medical researchers, they wanted to know what it was and how it worked in order to better find remedies and cures for it. The purpose of this book is not to bog us down in sin or overwhelm us with a sense of failure, but to prompt desires for health and promote responses that bring healing.

Speaking of the tradition, the account I offer in this book is my own appropriation of historical Christian thinking, from the early-fourth-century Christian ascetic communities in the deserts of Egypt (collected in *The Sayings of the Desert Fathers*) to St. Augustine, and through the Middle Ages. I'm especially interested in the work of the medieval theologian Thomas Aquinas, since he is the focus of my scholarly research, and he tries to bring together all the voices of the Christian tradition before him into a single account. Because he is a synthetic thinker, he also appreciates and critically engages the Greek philosophical tradition sometimes interwoven with those voices. There is a dialectical pattern in his work that I hope is also reflected in my own. While my discussion in this book is in no small part a reflection of my conversation with Aquinas and his forebears, like Aquinas, I take my contribution to be a spur to further reflection on the subject, not the final word.

With that frame in mind, we can shine the spotlight on vainglory. In Chapters One and Two, I'll explain vainglory's status in Christian tradition as a "capital vice" (or deadly sin). This will help explain why our desires for glory can go so deeply and badly wrong. Then I'll analyze vainglory's definition — in two parts. First, what is "glory," and is it really a good thing, especially for Christians? Second, how do we seek "glory" in morally twisted ways, both on account of vain things and for vain purposes?

After explaining what vainglory is, I'll explore in Chapter Three the ways this vice can be rooted both in pride and in fear. The Christian tradition distinguishes pride from vainglory, but also explores the close motivational links between the two. Put briefly, the prideful desire superiority, and the vainglorious desire the *show* of superiority, although these can easily be entangled in practice. (That fact partly explains, I think, why the two vices were merged into one on later lists of the deadly sins, and why the English term "vanity" captures the flavor of both.) However, I argue that, in addition to pride, we should add fear to the motivations that can spark vainglorious tendencies. In fact, St. Augustine's life story, as he tells it in the *Confessions,* provides vivid examples of vainglory in both its prideful and its fearful forms.

In Chapter Four, I expand our view from vainglory's roots upward toward its fruits or offshoot vices, which illustrate its propensity to spawn other vices. These offspring vices will lead us to questions about truthfulness in self-display. How can we handle worries about hypocrisy when practicing virtue? How is truthfulness in self-display threatened by the incentives that vainglory offers to conceal ourselves? There's a lot at stake here, since our greatest friendships and even our fulfillment depend on commitments to truthful self-communication.

In Chapter Five, I'll explore the way that genuine excellence in virtue can degenerate into the desire for empty applause. The ancient virtue of magnanimity ("greatness of soul") articulates well the attractive and attention-getting power of goodness. How can we slide from genuine virtue down the slippery slope to the mere veneer of virtue, and then to sheer attention-mongering? It takes work to keep from sliding into pride on the one side of this virtue and from settling for a sham reputation of one's once and former glory on the other. A closer look at those who have outstanding and remarkable excellence articulates the struggles of those who live in the spotlight. When we stand in such a position, how can we keep our focus and not get sidetracked by the seductive addiction to applause?

In Chapter Six I canvas remedies and spiritual disciplines recommended by the Desert Fathers and others in the Christian tradition for resisting vainglorious temptations. Relying on the power of grace, with Christ-like character as our goal, we can submit ourselves to God's transforming power through practices of silence and solitude. And when those avenues are not open to us, we can learn to gratefully and gracefully handle positions which bring us glory. A sermon by St. Augustine models how this can be done together as a community.

Lastly, in Chapter Seven, I consider questions that arise from the discussion of vainglory so far. First, when we talk about vices, our need for God's grace to resist them sometimes feels like it stands in tension with our own efforts to change our bad habits. If we frame our pursuit of virtue and our resistance to vice in ways that give divine agency — God's grace and forgiveness — its due, how can we avoid "cheap grace" and leave room for Christian practices and spiritual discipline? On the other hand, if we stress spiritual disciplines, how do we avoid temptations to "works righteousness"? Second, once we start thinking about vainglory, it might seem impossible for Christians to "build each other up in love" without making the one we're building up vulnerable to this vice. If vainglory typically takes the form of a social vice, one in which there is an actor and an audience, are there positive social practices — inside and outside the church — in which we can offer another encouragement and affirm another's goodness without tempting him or her to vainglory? And finally, if you're not a Christian, what's so bad about enhancing your own reputation? If all glory is good only insofar as it points ultimately to God as the source of all goodness, should we expect those who don't believe in God to recognize vainglory — in any of its forms — as a vice?

Answering these questions and addressing the power of vainglory in our lives leads us, of course, beyond the pages of a book and back into practical matters. More than a decade ago, my family moved to the city where we now live and began looking for a new church home. As we entered one church's narthex, my daughter — then a toddler — drew in an audible breath of wonder. "What is it?" we asked her. Looking all around her, she answered, "This church has *such* beautiful carpeting!" She was right — its vivid color and bold pattern were immediately eye-catching. Through its plush floor covering, the narthex proclaimed itself a place of luxury. I was a bit nonplussed to think that our first impressions of that place were riveted on the church's affluent *appearance* rather than something of spiritual significance. (In some cathedrals, by contrast, the exquisitely wrought architecture is designed to point attention heavenward — in contrast to that carpet, which kept our focus downward toward material things.) Perhaps that's not fair, since spiritual beauty is usually something that takes more than a first impression to notice, and many treasures are held in jars of clay. Still, we wondered if this church's beautiful virtue would outshine their beautiful carpet, and — more importantly — whether that isn't a kind of metaphor for a question all of us might usefully consider. A spiritually beautiful life is something we gradually grow into, even as we learn to shun its flashier vainglorious substitutes. There is warning here, and a task. As Shakespeare once put it, "How like Eve's apple doth thy beauty grow/If thy sweet virtue answer not thy show."[8]

CHAPTER 1

GLORY, GOODNESS, AND GETTING ATTENTION

Glory follows virtue as if it were its shadow.
{Gloria virtutem tanquam umbra sequitur.}

Cicero, *Tusculan Disputations*

AUGUSTINE'S *Confessions* IS a classic story in which he confesses his own sin and professes God's faithfulness. Although I'd assigned the book in my classes for years, not until I started researching vainglory did I register how strong and recurrent a theme this vice is in Augustine's life. Augustine struggled with vainglory in every single form I will outline in this chapter. Reflecting on his struggle, I realized how common it is. To tell Augustine's story of vainglory is to tell our own.

Having a name for a vice is like having a medical diagnosis. It gives us a clearer idea of what we're facing, helps us disentangle surface symptoms from root causes, and points to remedies or therapies that are likely to be most effective. We've already seen vainglory's embarrassingly familiar face — on Facebook and in the front pews. While the Christian tradition offers us a name for and a definition of this vice, Augustine gives it a personal portrait and a narrative. With the help of this wisdom from the past, in the next two chapters I'll translate this source of temptation and trouble for our time.

The *Confessions* opens with these words:

Great are you, O Lord, and greatly to be praised; great is your power and your infinite wisdom. Human beings, as but a little part of your creation, would praise you; human beings who bear with them their mortality, the witness of their sin, the witness that you resist the proud. Yet they would praise you; they, who are but a part of your creation. You wake us to delight in your praise; for you made us for yourself, and our hearts are restless, until they rest in you.[1]

Like Augustine, we'll focus first on the greatness of God and the goodness of his creation as worthy of glory. In this chapter we'll ask, What is glory and when is it good? Then, in the next chapter, we'll look at the ways sin spoils glory by severing right relationships between goodness and glory. That is, we'll explore what makes glory *vain*. We'll work in this order because vices always name good things gone wrong. We can understand sin's damage more clearly if we look first at how good God created things to be.

Good Glory?

If you are a Christian today, when you hear the term "glory," you may well assume that glory is something that only God can rightly have.[2] That means that *any* glory human beings could seek or have as their own is, by definition, disordered. And Scripture does speak clearly about glory belonging to God. In Psalm 19 the poet writes, "The heavens declare the glory of God" (Ps. 19:1); the great hymns recorded in Revelation proclaim God's glory (Rev. 19:1, 7); Christ himself directs his disciples to do their good deeds for the glory of God the Father (Matt. 5:16; John 15:8), and claims that in his glory the Father is glorified (John 13:31). In fact, almost all positive references to glory in Scripture are to *God's* glory. Human beings, on the other hand, are warned, condemned, and punished for glory-seeking, from the Old Testament kings and the ostentatiously rich admonished by the prophets to the Pharisees of Jesus' day and the false apostles trying to outdo Paul in the New Testament.

Contemporary Christians who doubt whether glory can be good for us are in distinguished company. It turns out that there are lots of thinkers in the Christian tradition who argue about which sorts of things are good for us. Their arguments range over *all* the so-called goods that are the objects of the seven capital vices, not just glory. For example, in disputes over the nature of greed, some early Christian thinkers thought that money could be used well without gradually corrupting our desires, while others believed that Christians should aspire to be completely detached from worldly possessions. John Cassian, an early spiritual writer (c. 360-435 A.D.) who studied spiritual discipline with the Desert Fathers, instructs monks to give up ownership of every last penny, lest their renunciation of worldly values be incomplete. His worry? Lingering desires for possessions leave a root from which serious spiritual problems can grow, such as dejection over one's vocation and chronic problems with wrath.[3] The stories of the Desert Fathers — the spiritual leaders of ascetic communities in the wildernesses of fourth-century Egypt — recall one monk who even gave away his Bible, reasoning that if the Bible commanded the rich young ruler to "give all he had to the poor and follow [Christ]," then the book giving him that instruction was itself included in "all he had."[4] Augustine, on the other hand, was more sanguine about the possession of wealth. He warned about excess but did not condemn owning private property altogether.[5]

Looking back in the tradition, we find similar disputes about the vice of wrath. Could Christians ever be angry in the right way for the right things (e.g., injustice), or should they leave vengeance only for the Lord? Cassian follows his teacher Evagrius (345-399 A.D.) in completely prohibiting anger at another human being because of its disruptive influence on prayer.[6] Theologian Thomas Aquinas (1224-1274 A.D.) takes a more moderate position, arguing that anger is an emotion that can be used well or badly, and in some cases gives us the energy needed to right a wrong. And then there's the centuries-long argument among celibate monks and theologians about whether sexual pleasure in marriage is good, or whether marital intercourse is permitted only as a necessary evil, and its pleasure regarded as a "remedy for concupiscence," tinted by shame.[7] As in the case of glory, most of the controversy revolved around how to most faithfully interpret scriptural teachings about what is good for human beings and when and why.

So, can glory ever be good for humans?

Here's where definitions can help. We need to note that "glory," as it is used in the tradition's discussion, often meant something much less theologically loaded than the term Christians today use most frequently in worship or prayer. Glory, as Aquinas defines it, simply means "goodness that is displayed." The annuals in my front yard bloom in profusion where my family and neighbors can see them; they are meant to be a lovely display. Even turning in a paper to your college professor might count as displaying your goodness to others (if it's a well-crafted paper, that is!). And if your professor uses your paper as a model for other students to emulate, she is displaying its goodness for still another audience.

What would it look like to accept Aquinas's description of glory as goodness that is made "apparent and manifest in its splendor"?[8] This description simply means that when people notice something good and recognize its attractiveness or desirability, they typically express approval and praise. The neighbors enjoy looking at my flowerbed of bright purple impatiens and remark to me how much they appreciate their beauty. The student's paper earns an A and a commendatory note on the back page from his professor.

I've begun with these examples to show that on this definition, the goodness in question does not have to be *moral* goodness. It can be anything that is good or that we perceive as good. The clearer and more manifest the goodness is, and the greater the goodness is, the more recognition and approval it typically elicits — as when your YouTube video goes viral and earns your garage band's new song vastly more "likes" than "dislikes." You can show your *own* goodness deliberately or without intending to do so, or *others* can call attention to it. Even if an artist is skeptical about the success of her latest creation, a gallery owner can recognize its genius and put it on display. In the right context, almost anything good created by God or made by us can attract notice. Its glory testifies to and affirms the goodness of the world God created, and of our own creative abilities when they imitate his. In short, if anything good is shown and known, we've got a case of glory.

Human goodness, too, extends beyond the realm of the moral. If we are thinking only about shows of moral or spiritual goodness, we could narrow the meaning of "glory seeking" to taking credit for our virtuous actions instead of giving credit to God and his grace and power. This is certainly one of the types of vainglory that Christians should be concerned about. But thinkers in the tradition meant something broader than this by "glory."

So any display of genuine goodness is a case of glory — whether human effort helped produce it or not. A glorious sunset over Lake Michigan is a palette of beautiful colors spread across the sky — evidence of beauty and goodness in the created world that we can see and appreciate. A virtuoso performance of Brahms' first piano concerto is also something that holds our attention and draws our applause, and rightly so. When novelist Anne Lamott writes wonderingly of her sleeping newborn son, "His hands are like little stars," his precious body, too, counts as a case of something glorious.[9] The conversation about glory in the Christian tradition starts with the display of all and any types of goodness, even the goodness of inanimate objects like sunsets, and then narrows to cases of attention given to human goodness generally, like a beautiful musical performance, and finally focuses on instances of human virtue or moral goodness as even more specific cases.

If glory means something good being put on display for others, then glory and the concept of beauty, especially visible attractiveness, are closely linked.[10] Both glory and beauty apply to a wide range of goods, moral and natural, from intentional actions to physical objects. Both "glory" and "beauty" evoke the idea of being something that draws our notice and appreciation. Similarly, in the moral life, we are attracted to certain exemplars — people whose lives display goodness that we admire and find attractive.

Aquinas uses the term "clarity" to explain how glory is goodness made manifest, and he is quick to point out that "glory" and "witness" are closely related. Bearing witness (e.g., to the gospel) is itself a case of making some good clearly known. Such witness is clearly a spiritual task, a task that — not accidentally — is done better when there is integrity between the goodness I'm preaching about and my own faithfulness in practicing it. When I am witnessing to the truth of something, both the quality of my witness and my motivation for bearing witness can be the subject of moral praise or blame. So, too, with glory. Just as witnessing can be done well or badly, so in a similar way our display of any other good can be done in healthy or disordered ways. This means, however, that human glory *can* be a good thing.

Of course, Aquinas's definition of glory — "goodness that is displayed" — also paradigmatically includes the way God has glory. God's goodness is shown and made known to us both in creation and in Scripture. God's is the most exemplary case of glory because there is no goodness beyond his and nothing vaster than its display.[11] It will also be important in Christian thinking about glory (and vainglory) that God's goodness is always the ultimate source of all other goodness. In its display, all other goodness, including any of ours, therefore reflects something of who God is.

Though goodness comes in a wide range of kinds, it's human goodness as it is shown and known — cases of human glory — that I'll focus on in the rest of this book, because they are the cases that typically get us into moral and spiritual trouble. So what can go wrong with human glory?

Honor Cultures and Glory-Seeking

Even if we are convinced by this broader definition that glory can *in theory* be a good for human beings, Christian suspicions of glory as a good are understandable, especially given the practices of glory-seeking among the cultures where Christianity first developed. Ancient Greek and Roman cultures unapologetically counted honor and glory among the primary human goods to seek and win for oneself. The ancient Greek philosopher Plato (427-347 B.C.) wrote a dialogue titled *Symposium* in which one character comments, "Look, if you will, at how human beings seek honor . . . wanting to become famous and 'to lay up glory immortal forever,' and how they're ready to brave any danger for the sake of this, much more than they are for their children; and they are prepared to spend money, suffer through all sorts of ordeals, and even die for the sake of glory."[12] In late antiquity, Augustine paints a similar picture of Roman motives in his magnum opus, *The City of God:* "But since those Romans were in an earthly city . . . in the sphere of demise and succession, where the dead are succeeded by the dying — what else but glory should they love, by which they wished even after death to live on in the mouths of their admirers?"[13]

As N. T. Wright points out, even when New Testament writers adopted the character-based focus of the ethical systems around them, they also had to innovate dramatically when marking *what sorts* of character traits counted as virtues. Although Jesus surely exemplified the Greek cardinal virtues, "What the earliest Christians were struck by . . . was that in Jesus they had seen . . . a way of being human which nobody had ever imagined before . . . a way which was both original in itself and the source of those other virtues that are commonly recognized as Christian innovations — namely, humility, charity, patience, and chastity."[14] The early Christians' strong reactions against the pride, honor, and glory-seeking of Greek and Roman moral paradigms reflected their commitment to making Christ and his humiliation their model of virtue.

As we try to be both discerning and innovative in our engagement with various cultures — whether ancient or contemporary — that get glory wrong, we need to distinguish honor-seeking and glory-seeking. If we confuse the two concepts, which are often used synonymously in ordinary conversation, this further complicates the assessment of glory as a good. If your name is great or you are famous, this usually implies both being respected or revered (honored) *and* being renowned or widely recognized for it (glorified). Mother Teresa, for example, long known for her work with the poor in Calcutta, won a Nobel Peace Prize, making her an icon for altruism worldwide. Her mercy to the poor is worthy of honor *and* it is well-known. Aquinas argues that honor and glory usually go together, since being respected and honored has glory as its natural effect: "Praise and honor . . . stand in relation to glory as causes from which it proceeds, so that glory is compared to them as their end. [One] reason why someone loves to be honored and praised is that one thinks one will acquire a certain renown in the knowledge of others in that way."[15] Do you want to be famous and go down in history? Accomplish something outstanding or worthy of notice. Win a major military victory, invent some life-saving device, create an amazing work of art or literature, or share wisdom by founding a school. Encouraging such endeavors seems wise for a society that gives attention to what is honorable. Contrast this with a society that encourages people to seek fame for just about anything at all, whether honorable or not.

Still, it can be hard for us to grasp the difference between honor and glory. Here's an example that might help. The city where I live — Grand Rapids, Michigan — holds an annual public art competition called ArtPrize. Tens of thousands of people mill around the downtown area for three weeks, where hundreds of pieces of art are displayed — everything from sculptures made of recycled tires set up in a parking lot, to glittering glass mosaics on the sides of buildings, to elaborate pencil sketches displayed on a wall in the art museum. Viewers vote for their favorite works of art during the first two weeks of the competition; then the public-vote tally and the choices of art critics determine the top ten entries. The winners each get a large cash prize. It is typical for installations that are large and spectacular to get a lot of buzz and news coverage, thousands of visitors, and an avalanche of votes; one year's competition featured an enormous flying pig the size of a small airplane, for example, that was seen and voted for by many. But greater attention does not always track higher quality, nor do excellently crafted pieces always win the most votes. The art critics' choices are sometimes very different from the public choices, though part of the fun of the competition is the interesting overlap — and the debates about what counts as art that ensue. The piece *honored* with first prize thus can be different from the piece that won the most votes in the early rounds of public opinion — an indicator of which got the most *glory*. Of course, the honor of being awarded first prize can subsequently also bring greater glory to an art piece if a bigger audience goes to see it because of its winning status. So the story of glory and honor is complicated and intertwined. To understand certain forms of vainglory, however, we'll have to be clear on the difference.

Defending the Goodness of Glory

We're in a better position now to answer our original question: How should Christians view human glory? Aquinas directly responds to Christians' concerns about glory being good.[16] He offers a double strategy. First, he answers Scripture with Scripture. He cites, for example, verses from the Sermon on the Mount to argue that we should want our good works to be seen by others (Matt. 5:14-16).[17] It would be hard to argue that seeking glory is morally suspect when Jesus himself commands his disciples to "let [their] light shine before others." This verse in Matthew is found less than a chapter before Jesus' warnings to his disciples to do their good deeds in secret, in contrast to the Pharisees' religious displays, which are designed to garner human glory, but which receive no reward from their Father in heaven (Matt. 6:1ff.; see also Matt. 23). This means that despite his awareness of the problems and temptations surrounding glory, Jesus still commends letting our light shine. In other passages, the apostle Paul both prohibits boasting and does some boasting "in the Lord" on his own behalf (contrast 1 Cor. 13:4 with 2 Cor. 10 and Jer. 9:23-24). Aquinas reconciles the texts in tension by offering a distinction from Augustine: in commendable cases, glory is sought for God's sake and directed to God; in cases that are condemned, glory is sought exclusively as one's own, with no reference to God. So the command to "let your light shine before others, so that they may see your good works" is immediately followed with "and give glory to your Father in heaven" (Matt. 5:16, NRSV).

Aquinas offers other reasons for thinking of glory as a good. Human beings have a natural desire to be known, he says, and more specifically, for their goodness to be known.[18] They are not unique in this respect, either, for they are also reflecting their Creator. Goodness, by its nature, tends to "communicate itself" to another.[19] Put more simply, like the "contagious" effect of a smile, and like sunshine, good things tend to overflow their source and share themselves. For example, God, the perfect good and origin of all goodness, shares his goodness through the act of creation. Although creating a good world was not necessary, there's something fitting about this act on God's part. His goodness has the character of a gift — something given to another as a sign of love. In creation, the reality God made good reveals his goodness. God also shares his goodness with human beings specifically through revelation. Here his goodness is revealed as truth — in *words,* not *things.* So, in general, the communication of one's goodness[20] — goodness clearly shown and known to others — so far from counting as morally suspect, should be what we expect, given the natural dynamics of goodness in a world made by such a God. Like point and counterpoint, goodness radiates outward like ripples on a pond, whereas beauty draws our attention in like a magnet draws iron filings. Human glory can be a kind of extension of God's glory, a creaturely imitation of God's goodness. In short, the sharing of goodness is natural and can be used in proper ways for proper ends. Thus there is a rightful place for glory — goodness shared through knowledge and communicated through display — as a good in human life.

Of course, the next question is this: How can the beauty we display appropriately draw attention to what is good? The purpose of *God's* glorious good deeds is to bring us closer to him. So also our good deeds can make God known to others and also help bring them closer to him. Like the "standing stones" the Israelites placed by the Jordan (Josh. 4:1-9), our actions can testify to a love beyond ourselves that we draw on in our otherwise ordinary daily work, attracting notice and admiration. This is how Aquinas interprets Jesus' Sermon on the Mount: "God seeks glory, not for His own sake, but for ours. In like manner, we may rightly seek our own glory for the good of others, according to Matthew 5:16, 'That they may see your good works and glorify your Father who is in heaven.'"[21] Our glory, says Aquinas, can be useful in glorifying God, and our example can be an encouragement and an incentive to others who "may become better by reason of the good they know to be in [us]."[22]

People often learn to be good by seeing the goodness of others displayed. So Paul writes, "Whatever you have learned or received or heard from me, or seen in me — put it into practice" (Phil. 4:9). Children learn to become good by imitating the parents, teachers, and mentors who serve as their role models. A few years ago, one of my boys added new phrases to his bedtime prayers shortly after he began second grade at the local Christian school. I wondered where he had learned them (or if he was making them up), so I e-mailed a few characteristic lines to his teacher to ask her if they sounded familiar. He was indeed quoting her prayers, prayers he'd heard her pray day after day in class and had copied into his prayer journal at school. His teacher thanked me for writing. "Sometimes I wonder if they are even listening," she wrote, "but I'm blessed to know that they are." We can see similar dynamics at play when we bear witness in the world and build up other members of the church. At its glorious best, our goodness is a gift to others.[23]

To Aquinas's arguments, I would add that having one's created goodness be known seems to be not only a fundamental human need, but also a prerequisite for genuine love and friendship. Witness the behavior of children, who regularly seek affirmation in verbal and non-verbal ways from their parents; conversely, notice the problems that come with neglect.[24] Small children often make eye contact with a parent when playing, as if the parent's attention is affirmation enough, and they cry out "Look at me!" when sitting at the top of the slide, as if the activity is worth doing for the attention it commands, which confirms the loving relationship between them. Similarly, consider that intermittent positive feedback from others usually tracks how satisfied and motivated most people feel doing a task or a job. As a teacher, I find that some positive evaluations from my students at the end of the semester often make the grading feel worthwhile — not because I need my work lauded for its own sake, but because I know my efforts were genuinely appreciated as good by those I was trying to serve.[25] Without any response from the students who profit from my efforts — even if their response is fallible — I am hampered in gauging my effectiveness and often feel less encouraged to press on or improve.

Consider one last but less obvious case. Couldn't knowing and acknowledging another *itself* be an expression of love? Attentiveness to others can be a gift that expresses love. In Scripture, a certain deep knowledge signals interpersonal love and union (see Gen. 4:1; Isa. 43; Ps. 139; Phil. 1:9-11): "Before you were born, I knew you."[26] One way that lovers communicate their feelings is by looking into each other's eyes — that is, by openly attending to each other. When my six-year-old child brings art home from school, my attention to the details of his creation is not so much a measure of his artistic talent (though it could be), but an affirmation of my love for him and my appreciation for his gift. Its display on our refrigerator signals a mutual love-exchange between us, expressed through the giving and receiving of positive attention — attention not so much for any specific achievements but for our very selves. These cases of recognition-giving or attention-giving as acts of love mirror God's act, the ultimate paradigm. As C. S. Lewis puts it,

> The sense that in this universe we are treated as strangers, the longing to be acknowledged, to meet with some response, to bridge some chasm that yawns between us and reality, is part of our inconsolable secret. And surely, from this point of view, the promise of glory, in the sense described, becomes highly relevant to our deep desire. For glory means good report with God, acceptance by God, response, acknowledgment, and welcome into the heart of things. The door on which we have been knocking all our lives will open at last.[27]

These practical examples show that human glory is *for* building relationships with others and signaling a creation-affirming love relationship with God. Therefore, glory cannot be a good for an individual alone. It is a gift and a sign for the sake of another. I'll return to this point in

Chapter Seven, when I address what sorts of practices of celebration and acknowledgment can foster encouragement without falling into vainglory.

Glorying Well

What does it mean to glory well? Clearly, "Let your light shine" does not mean "Always shine, never blend." Human glory may be a genuine good, but our pursuit of it can still go wrong. In the words of D. L. Moody, "Lighthouses do not ring bells and fire cannons to call attention to their shining — they just shine."[28] How do we shine *well*?

If glory is genuinely good, it is still a good we are susceptible to love in mistaken and malformed ways. Why is glory a source of seduction for us? Why are we so drawn to glory that its allure outshines our love for God? Why are we so tempted to organize our whole lives around seeking and finding it?

Human beings are social creatures. We need to live in relationships with each other. If we are to be known and loved, we must be acknowledged, affirmed, and appreciated for who we are and for the good that we do — in fact, it is essential to our fullest well-being. And according to the tradition, being known and loved and knowing and loving others are what human beings were made for — Aquinas calls it "the fellowship of eternal happiness." Good human community requires attentiveness to and affirmation of others. That's true of parenting, friendship, mentoring, and our relationships with larger groups. The ancient Greek philosopher Aristotle (384-322 B.C.) says that to be friends, you have to wish good things to another, but you must also be aware of and appreciate the good in your friend, as your friend does in you.[29] In short, when communities offer their members the right sorts of mutual attentiveness and affirmation, people flourish.

For evidence, we need look no further than the damage done to those people who do not have this good. When they are invisible or ignored, or when their real goodness is denied or devalued by others, they are hurt. Neglected children show us this painful condition, and so do lives marred by sexist or racist treatment, or even abuse. Something good in them has *not* been seen, *not* been acknowledged, *not* been valued and appreciated as good. Missing is glory for the goodness they have — a glory none of us can live well without.

There's also something in human recognition that gives us a foretaste of the glory to come, according to C. S. Lewis. He says,

> I am not forgetting how quickly the lawful pleasure of praise from those whom it is my duty to please turns into the deadly poison of self-admiration. But I thought I could detect a moment during which the satisfaction of having pleased those whom I rightly loved and rightly feared was pure. And that is enough to raise our thoughts to what may happen when the redeemed learn at last that we have pleased Him whom we were created to please. There will be no room for vanity then. We will most innocently rejoice in the thing God has made us to be.[30]

Precisely because such glory is so necessary and beneficial to human flourishing, I believe there are two fatal substitutions that we are tempted to make. First, rather than experiencing human recognition and praise as a foretaste of God's, or as God communicating approval to us through another, we make humanly given glory our ultimate end. We try to ground our egos and identities on the fickle foundation of human approval and affirmation, recognition and reward. Perhaps we are liable to fall into this trap because, when human feedback regarding our worth comes, it seems more tangible and readily evident than God's acknowledgment of it.

Second, we tend to confuse two types of human recognition, which philosophers call "recognition self-respect" and "appraisal self-respect."[31] Appraisal self-respect is the recognition and approval we receive on the basis of our particular accomplishments or performances. "Sarah, that was such an uplifting performance! You must have practiced very hard; the music just seemed to flow through your violin strings." It is merit-based attention from others, and it is conditional on our efforts and achievements. Recognition self-respect, on the other hand, is the underlying recognition and approval that we are worthy of simply as human beings. "Sam, I know that performance wasn't what you'd hoped for this time, but I want you to know that I love you regardless of how you played today." This form of regard is unconditional and dependent only on our humanity — that is, the ineradicable dignity we bear as those created in God's image — not on our achievements, notable or otherwise.

Although it's all very well to distinguish these in principle, anyone who has ever been assessed or had to assess others knows that these two are very hard to distinguish in experience. An assessment of my performance can *feel* like an assessment of my person, especially if I have poured my heart into my work and have a deep investment in what I have done. When a professor receives a really negative and critical review, for example, it's much easier for her to think that she's a lousy philosopher than to think that this particular article wasn't such a great piece of philosophical writing. When a parent criticizes a child who talks back, the child is more likely to think "My dad thinks I'm terrible" rather than "My dad really doesn't appreciate my smart mouth." Messages of affirmation and condemnation are powerful; it takes effort and experience to disconnect the person and the performance, the agent and the accomplishment.[32]

As the early Christian monks will teach us in Chapter Six, if we are secure in the recognition self-respect we have from God, then we can better shrug off or rightly accept human assessments, whether they are affirming or not. But if we are not secure in that unconditional sense of worth, we may seek recognition self-respect from human beings, trying to build secure self-acceptance on the shaky foundation of human opinion. Compounding that first substitution error, we may further try to win human appraisals of our *achievements* and use them to shore up that weak foundation, hoping that enough conditional approval will somehow be transformed into a solid and enduring core of self-worth. Like a teenager's obsessive investment in the latest fashion to earn popularity with his friends, this amounts to building a flimsy house on shifting sand, not rock-solid acceptance. All this is just to point out that vainglory is a human habit as easy to make as it is hard to break.

Vainglory's deep appeal drives us to seek attention in many disordered ways. In the next chapter, I'll catalog its many faces — from flaunting it to faking it.

CHAPTER 2

VARIETIES OF VAINGLORY

Glory is fleeting; obscurity is forever.

Napoleon Bonaparte

O UR ATTACHMENTS TO glory, though sometimes good, can very easily go bad. When teaching about vainglory, I have often called this the "A.A.A." vice — an acronym for Attention, Affirmation, and Applause (or Acknowledgment, Approval, and Adulation — take your pick). Besides describing the vice, the A.A.A. acronym can also help us analyze the moral features of a vainglorious act. First, what are we getting glory for? Anything? Or something truly good? Second, why are we attached to it? Because it's all about us and our addiction to being the center of attention? And lastly, by whom are we seeking to be recognized? Audience will matter, too. In fact, analyzing who your intended audience is often usefully illuminates what particular good you will put on display, and why you are trying to get attention.

For example, if I were trying to impress an audience of philosophers, I could use a sophisticated vocabulary, name-drop authors I've read lately, and mention important thinkers in my professional network. Choosing to put these things — good in themselves — on display enhances my own reputation with this audience as an academically astute thinker. Why do I want this audience's approval? Because my ability to get tenure or publish or gain professional success depends on their positive assessment.

The tradition summed up disordered pursuits of glory by calling them "vain," meaning "empty." (The Latin *vana gloria* and the Greek *cenodoxia* both literally mean glory that's empty.) If good things are worthy of glory, then "empty" things lack goodness, or, at the very least, don't deserve the amount of glory they get. Glory is a problem in two main ways, according to Aquinas. First, glory can be sought for "vain" or empty things — like the wealth showcased on Robin Leach's *Lifestyles of the Rich and Famous*. And second, glory can be sought "in vain," that is, for a trivial or selfish (or even morally bad) purpose — as when the cover of *Vanity Fair* featured a pair of shirtless soccer-player stars: the display of their buff bodies aimed to incite lust and increase magazine sales. Glory goes bad when we desire it for the wrong things and for the wrong ends. Those things or ends are "empty" of the goodness that matches the glory they're given (or the glory we want them to be given). The glory here is a veneer; it does not have the requisite substance of goodness beneath it. Aquinas and other Christian thinkers distinguish the forms of vainglory by the categories of "object" and "motive": roughly translated, *what* we glory in and *why*.

Vain Objects

First, let's consider vainglory's object: *what* we are seeking or getting recognition and affirmation for. There are several ways our glory can be vain. Think of the businessman who might fake expertise in a public talk or a professional task. In one cartoon, an office professional stands before a committee with a chart and admits, "At this juncture in my presentation, I'd like to dispense with the illusion of coherence."[1] Or consider the case of a woman who undergoes plastic surgery because she thinks she'll never be attractive enough without it, or a teenager who spends an inordinate amount of money keeping up with the latest fashions. These people are pursuing glory for fake stuff and fluff — for goodness they don't have and for goodness that isn't worth getting attention for. Under the category of "vain things," these are the first two ways our lives become marked by a disordered love of glory.

Let's consider each of these cases in a bit more detail. Faking goodness is, of course, the most extreme case of seeking glory vainly, because the "goodness" you're displaying is in fact nothing more than a false or an empty show: there's no goodness there — only the appearance of it. Examples of this type of vainglory include the highly embellished resumé, the eternally youthful hair color, the wise nods of students pretending to understand their philosophy professors, the clean room effected by shoving all the clutter into a remote drawer or closet, the fudging of golf scores when recounting a recent game, the carefully Photoshopped professional photograph, and the tale of "the one that got away" on the last fishing trip.

What we get glory for can be vain in another way, as when, even if you *do* have it, the goodness in question is not terribly worthy of attention or acknowledgment: it's fluff. Perhaps it's something really shallow or superficial. It could, however, be something more serious and socially respectable, although not, in the grand scheme of life, all that important. As a third, paradoxical case, it can even be something bad or immoral that is nonetheless regarded as remarkable. (Although such an evil quality is also not worthy of glory, it is neither a faked nor a good quality, so it counts as a distinct case.)

On the superficial side, you can pull up to the stoplight in your pimped-up Escalade, or sport wild tattoos, lots of bling, and a great tan. Or you can be the person who is constantly getting calls on his cell phone and who needs everyone in the airport terminal to know about his conversation. Or you can be the first to have the latest cool app for your iPhone; you can have the best-manicured lawn in the neighborhood or the most perfectly decorated house; you can be an expert about obscure but awesome rock bands. Or you can have a large following on Twitter; you can have chili peppers behind your name on RateYourProfessor.com; you can win social credibility by wearing shirts from Abercrombie instead of Goodwill when you're in high school and shirts from Goodwill instead of Abercrombie when you're in college.

On the socially respectable side, you can be vainglorious by displaying all the conventional markers of personal and professional success: for example, having children with outstanding S.A.T. scores; having an impressive LinkedIn profile; putting important-sounding titles in your electronic signature line and listing strings of professional degrees behind your name; having a carefully cultivated reputation for eloquence in your sermons or erudition in your lectures; pasting stickers on your car window for every elite athletic team your children join; or being a college that advertises its top rank among liberal arts institutions of higher education in *U.S. News and World Report*.

Ironically, you can often show yourself to be socially respectable by displaying yourself as someone who is *not* committing the shallower forms of vainglory. For example, in certain communities legendary for valuing thrift and frugality such as the one I belong to, when you compliment me on my suit, it's a golden opportunity for me to let you know that I found the top designer brand for a bargain price on a sale rack. In this scenario, I have made sure you know I'm *not* one of those crass consumers who will spend tons of money at the mall in slavish service to her fashionable appearance. Rather, I am one of those clever people who is both a woman of taste and a conscientious steward of my financial resources. According to this more subtle vainglorious scheme, congratulations are still expected, but now twice over: first, I want to win approval for not being a shallow vainglorious person, and second, I want to win the social rewards of painstakingly cultivated respectability.

If, however, you can't be good in either a shallow or a socially respectable way, don't worry. There is still another way to glory in "vain things." This last form of vainglory I call the "Notorious Vainglorious" category. Think scenes from *The Godfather* here. In cases of glorying in notoriety, you win attention for things that are evil but that somehow still inspire rapt attention and awe in the relevant audience. Notorious vainglorious cases include engaging in locker-room talk and sexting, wickedly witty public ridicule of those in opposing political parties, and crazy public stunts of the *Fear Factor* variety; having the grossest and goriest Halloween costume, boasting about binge-drinking last weekend, and open rule-flouting that trumpets what cool rebels and non-conformists we are. The key here is not only to be bad, but to be publicly and impressively so. (This form of vainglory is likely made possible by human beings' fascination with evil, which also points to possible problems with the audience we have in mind.) Cassian has notorious vainglorious types in mind when he says, "You must not let yourself be flattered by your virtues or puffed up by the spiritual successes on your right, nor wander off to the path of vice on your left, and according to the Apostle, look there for glory in your shame."[2]

You may suspect that I'm having fun with these examples of vainglory, even though some of them clearly indict me, too. True enough. But note that all the examples I offer are only *possible* (though likely) cases of vainglory; they need not illustrate this vice in every instance. For all I know, there could be a range of motives, good and bad, mixed into any given action. Even if it were possible to plumb the depths of human motivation, I would not have time to sort out all the motives of any given action here. My point here is to warn us against rushing to overly simple judgments, because for all its outer behavioral symptoms, vainglory is primarily a vice — a habit of the *heart,* sometimes carefully hidden within us. That's why this analysis is mainly for self-examination, not for judging others.

Vain Objectives

Cases of glorying in vain things are the easy ones. They concern false, superficial, or suspicious claims to glory — when we desire acknowledgment for goods we don't really have or for goods that aren't worthy of that much attention or for attractive evils that draw an audience's awe when they should repel us. As the hymn writer puts it, they name "all the vain things that charm me most."[3] Such cases of vainglory tend to be easy to spot, easy to condemn, and provide endless fodder for quick cultural criticism. Unfortunately, they do not tell the whole story of vainglory.

By contrast, the second main form of vainglory concerns *truly* glory-worthy goods. In these cases of vainglory, we genuinely do have something good (there's no fakery), and those goods are genuinely worthy of applause (they are not fluff or fascinating evil stuff). Even in these cases, however, our attachment to the glory we receive for our goodness can still go morally awry. This way of glorying "in vain" concerns our ultimate motives, and I suspect that it lies behind all the other ways of glorying vainly.

I'll divide glorying "in vain" into two types of cases: a secular one and a saintly one. Augustine offers us a paradigm of the secular case in his well-known critique of the Romans in his book *The City of God.* He begins by lauding the impressive virtues of the Romans and cataloging the civic and military achievements made possible by their courage and temperance. In these respects, their renown is justly deserved. Then, however, Augustine takes his analysis one step deeper. What motivated their great feats of virtue? His answer: "Glory they most ardently loved: for it they wished to live, for it they did not hesitate to die."[4] In other words, their courageous victories and masterful civilization-building feats were for the sake of making their own names great, immortalizing themselves in the hearts and minds of others. Augustine argues that the proximity of the temples that the Romans built to the goddesses of Virtue and Honor is no accident. The real goodness of the Romans was corrupted because it was enacted for their own reputation. All their virtuous deeds ultimately served their love of praise and glory.

Augustine distinguishes between the city of God and the city of this world on just this point:

> Accordingly, two cities have been formed by two loves: the earthly city by the love of self, even to the contempt of God; the heavenly by the love of God, even to the contempt of self. The former, in a word, glories in itself; the latter in the Lord. For the one seeks glory from [human beings]; but the greatest glory of the other is God, the witness of conscience. The one lifts up its head in its own glory; the other says to its God: "You are my glory, and the lifter of my head."[5]

The problem, according to Augustine, is not only that the Romans sought to be virtuous for the sake of being famous, but also that they enjoyed their glory as something entirely their own. This is the "it's all about me" problem with glory. Why is this wrong? According to Augustine, it's not just selfish; it's idolatrous. To make themselves the ultimate locus of praise was prideful. The Romans didn't, or wouldn't, recognize that their virtue was a gift — that all goodness worthy of glory comes from God. Human glory is derivative; it is meant to point us back to the source of all goodness. To take God's glory for ourselves is, therefore, to rob God of what he is justly due.[6]

It would be a relief if Christians could congratulate themselves on this point, noting that they are not secular self-glory seekers. But it's not that simple. Christians struggle with this form of vainglory, too: there is a "saintly" version of glorying "in vain." In fact, temptations to vainglory may well be *worse* for the genuinely virtuous person. For those who make real progress in virtue, vainglory becomes more of a possible downfall, not less of one. Why? Good people are truly worthy of the renown and approval they get. Their goodness makes them more likely to receive recognition and praise from others, because outstanding character, virtue, and sanctity naturally attract attention.[7] Aquinas identifies the progression: The better you become, the more recognition typically comes your way; and the more recognition that comes your way, the more susceptible you can become to expecting it and becoming excessively attached to it — to wanting your goodness to be recognized, noticed, affirmed. This is not a temptation that afflicts only Roman statesmen. Speaking to his fellow monks, Cassian warns,

> We shall lose the fruits of all the works that we have accomplished at the behest of vainglory [because] we wronged God by preferring to do for the sake of human beings what we should have done for his sake. [Thus we are] convicted by him who knows what is hidden of having preferred human beings to God, and the glory of the world to the glory of God.[8]

Be especially careful when you are good, Cassian writes, for "We are in danger of falling [into vainglory] when we are victorious [over sin] and particularly after triumph."[9]

Imagine that you are a monk who hears that advice from Cassian. When you go back to your spiritual disciplines and prayers and Scripture reading, you face a dilemma: If you undertake these labors openly, you run the risk of others noticing any spiritual progress that you make and giving you glory for it. Then you will have to worry about getting too attached to having that attention, knowing that vainglory is "enlivened . . . by the virtuous successes of the one whom it assails."[10] On the other hand, if you keep your virtue a "hidden treasure"[11] because of your concern for vainglory, you know that this also is something good that you're doing, and you can congratulate *yourself* for doing such a good job of resting on the approval of God alone. Cassian's teacher Evagrius sums up the problem: "It is difficult to escape the thought of vainglory, for what you do to rid yourself of it becomes a new source of vainglory."[12]

The trouble in these sorts of cases is that the slide toward vainglory starts from being good. Cassian's metaphor is striking: "Such is the enemy's [i.e., the devil's] clever subtlety that it causes the soldier of Christ, whom he could not overcome with hostile arms [i.e., the vices], to fall by his own weapons [i.e., his own virtues]."[13] Aquinas describes this process as a degenerative one in which we move from desiring virtue to desiring that others respect us for it to simply desiring recognition and renown, whether it attaches to virtue anymore or not.

Glory Stories

Two stories illustrate such a progression. In his book *Fame Junkies,* Jake Halpern offers the instructive example of a professor of media studies at a contemporary university. This professor built a solid and respectable academic reputation by authoring several scholarly books on the history and psychology of television. He contributed valuable research to his field, and he loved teaching. When reporters sought an expert on that topic, this professor became the point-person for an informed opinion. Word got around that he interviewed well, with the result that he now regularly does interviews for major television news shows. He describes how it all started: "My main motivation for doing all these interviews was to extend my classroom, reach a wider audience, and create a broader public discourse [about the nature of television's impact on our culture]."[14] As he found himself being called more and more frequently and enjoying the interviews, he confessed to being motivated

> by the much more raw desire to be acknowledged. . . . As academics, we like to play that down, but I think what I do is really the ultimate scam: I get my own fame by trying to expose the psyche of other people who want fame. But being a professor, this is the only possible route I have. At the age of forty-five, I know I can't sing, dance, or be a sports star. . . .[15]

Halpern reports that one result of the professor's fame is that he now has a spacious office with grand views of the campus. After all, if the university is going to be on television, it wants to make good on that public relations opportunity, too. The new office includes a dressing room. As the professor puts it, "I recognize that the reason I have the biggest office, an endowed chair, and a good salary has less to do with the books I have written and more to do with the fact that the university is as obsessed with attention as everybody else."[16]

The interview reveals that the professor recognizes the progression of his desire for fame; like an addiction, his need for it keeps ramping up to higher and higher levels. Halpern writes, "This professor seems most aware of his own craving for attention in those dry periods when no news organizations call him. 'I haven't had a TV interview since the 17th of March,' the professor reported. 'And since then there have been moments when I've gotten worried that my career is over. Of course I'm being a bit hyperbolic, but this stuff is a little like heroin. I guess once you get used to a certain degree of attention, you need more, so you build up a tolerance, and I think there is no end to where this spiral could go.'" But the 17th of March was only two weeks ago, Halpern reminded him. "'No,'" replied the professor gravely, "'If it was just two weeks ago I wouldn't be worried. It was *three* weeks ago.'"[17]

How does vainglory become a habit? Through a process like this: Because of glory's association with goodness, vainglory can insidiously begin when we do great things and win respect for them, which typically brings us public recognition and renown. So the vainglorious person is often someone who begins by valuing a good thing or quality which wins her respect and attention. As time goes on, she grows to anticipate and expect others' positive feedback. She easily gets more and more attached to her audience and their reactions to her goodness. Being respected and acclaimed feels good! Her tendency to value the goodness that was her original focus erodes as the center of value slowly shifts toward the attention she gets for it. A community's high expectations for the person to deliver more great achievements (in virtue or something else) can create pressure. She may even become willing to sacrifice integrity here and there to maintain her reputation, even when she can't quite pull it off on a given occasion, compromising her original view of what was truly valuable. Over time she may resort to faking her goodness or showing off more ephemeral goods in order to keep the same level of attention coming. At this point the vainglorious person primarily desires an audience — *any* audience. The disordered desire for glory has gradually trumped other valuable goods. Glory-seeking is emptiest and most debased when it has come entirely loose from the goodness of its object and is sought merely for its own sake.

Cassian tells a similar vainglory story about a fourth-century desert monk. In this story, however, those giving the monk recognition for his virtuous achievements were not a real television audience but an imagined church congregation.

A bit of background will be helpful for understanding this story. The ascetic achievements and heroic virtue of the desert monks in Egypt during Cassian's lifetime had become widely known. Like the rich young ruler who sought out Jesus, people from all around the Mediterranean made pilgrimages to the deserts to seek counsel from a Desert Father renowned for his asceticism or to hear the wise reflections on Scripture of a monk known for his wisdom. "Give me a word, Abba," they would say. Sometimes desert monks of great repute for their spiritual achievements would be pressured to leave their desert hermitages to serve an important congregation in the city. Monks who joined the monastic movement and made great progress in sanctity, then, were well aware that their saintly virtue would bring renown, and with it, the temptation to forsake the vows of world renunciation that had brought them into the desert in the first place.

Here is Cassian's story:

I remember a certain old man from the time when I was living in the desert of Skete. He was going to a certain brother's cell to pay him a visit. When he got near the door, he heard the monk inside muttering something. Wanting to know what he was reading from Scripture or what, as the custom is, he was going over from memory, the older man stood at the door for a little while. And when this most devout interloper focused his hearing and listened more carefully, he discovered that the younger monk within was so much at the mercy of vainglory's onslaught as to believe that he was in a church exhorting a congregation with a magnificent sermon. And when the old man, still standing near, heard him finish his discourse and then announce the dismissal of the catechumens, he at once knocked on the door. The younger monk came out, greeting the old man with the customary reverence and bringing him in. Since he realized that he had been caught up in a fantasy and was troubled by this, he asked how long ago the older man had come, knowing he would be scandalized if his brother had heard him "preaching." The older man replied in a pleasantly amused manner: "I only arrived . . . when you were announcing the dismissal of the catechumens."[18]

Vain motives can corrupt us when we get glory for vain things or virtuous things, and they can plague celebrities and Christian saints alike. Whether your glorious goods are real or imagined, and whether your audience is real or imagined, excessive attachment to your own glory can often present a moral danger. One thinker in the tradition put it well: "While other vices find their abode in the servants of the devil, vainglory finds a place even in the servants of Christ."[19]

A Capital Vice

No wonder that, according to the tradition, vainglory is no ordinary vice. In fact, vainglory counted as one of "the capital vices." (I'll explain in a moment why I prefer this label to "the seven deadly sins.") Considering vainglory as a capital vice helps distinguish it from its close cousin pride, and shows why vainglory so easily becomes a deep character flaw and a problem that pervades so much of our lives.

The list of capital vices first emerged in the fourth century A.D. among communities of desert monks in Egypt. Evagrius of Pontus included vainglory on his list of eight vices (or, as he called them, "evil thoughts"), likely the first written record of the set that eventually became the seven deadly sins.[20] In fact, vainglory made Evagrius's unofficial top three, because his monastic community explicitly modeled their lives after Christ's solitary sojourn in the desert wilderness to face the temptations of the devil, recorded in Matthew 4 and Luke 4. These desert Christians read the three temptations of Christ as cases of gluttony, vainglory, and avarice (or pride). In their interpretation, the three temptations of Christ in the desert mirrored Adam and Eve's encounter with the serpent in the Garden (Genesis 3). Precisely where Adam and Eve fell into temptation and vice, Christ — the model of virtuous human perfection — proved victorious. The devil tempts Jesus with vainglory when he brings him to the top of the Temple Mount — a maximally visible place — and tells him to throw himself down so that everyone will gasp in awe at the armies of angels swooping down to save him, lest he strike his foot against a stone. In Evagrius's telling, the temptation for Christ is "that if he would listen to [the devil] he would be glorified for having suffered no harm from a fall" (Luke 4:1-13).[21]

Evagrius's disciple, John Cassian, in turn devoted a chapter to vainglory in his *Institutes of the Monastic Life and the Remedies for the Eight Principal Faults,* along with chapters on the other seven vices. The chapter on vainglory immediately precedes the final chapter on pride, since the two vices are closely related. Cassian's *Institutes* (along with Benedict's *Rule,* published between 510 and 580 A.D.) was a formative text and an authoritative charter for much of Western monasticism throughout the Middle Ages. Gregory the Great (540-604 A.D.) officially endorsed the list of eight vices in his widely read work on the book of Job, the *Moralia in Iob.* Gregory later became pope, which gave his writings additional authority and a wider audience. Through these key voices, the list of vices and vainglory's place on it became canonical.

Contrary to common opinion today, the capital vices were not originally singled out as being the worst possible sins or the ones that were the hardest to cure or the ones that would put you on the fast track to hell. In fact, the label "deadly sins" (also known as "mortal sins," in contrast to "venial sins") came into use centuries later. Cassian first called them "principal vices" *(principia vitia).* Later on, Aquinas would describe them with the Latin term *caput,* which means "head" (its Latin genitive form *capitis* is the root of our English word "capital"). Aquinas does not mean "head" as in "capital punishment," in which you might *lose* your head; rather, "head" indicates a source or fountainhead, the way we might talk about the head of a stream from which the rest flows. Gregory the Great also called the capital vices "heads" in the sense of being "director generals" of "a howling army" of other vices; the capital vices are the commanders with the overview of the battle who direct all the other foot-soldier vices to carry out their plans. And their plans, according to Gregory, are "to lay waste to your heart." The capital or commanding vices fight on behalf of pride, the "queen" of the vices.[22]

When preparing for battle, it is worth knowing your enemy's strategy. That way you can develop a counter-strategy, fight back more effectively, and avoid surprise attacks. So Evagrius, Cassian, and Gregory try to catalog the ways vainglory and its minions attempt to conquer us (like C. S. Lewis imagines the demons' plots in *The Screwtape Letters*) in order that we can be on guard and better resist them. Whether we call them principal or capital or commanding vices, the picture we get from the early tradition is of certain main vices being the source of many others that come in their wake, directing them all toward a sinful agenda.

The point of calling them *vices* rather than *sins* is to note that we are talking about dispositional *patterns* of thought, feeling, and behavior, not individual actions. We're concerned about the way sin accumulates into bad habits of character, the way repeated actions can form or deform us, the way our vision and motivation are shaped by a thousand small steps. Talking about vainglory and all the rest as vices helps us see that individual sins interconnect to form patterns of sin that warp our character over a lifetime.

Searching in Vain for Happiness

Why did early Christian thinkers single out these particular vices as capital? Their point was to identify the sinful patterns of disordered loves we could build a life around — desirable goods that tempt us to seek happiness in them, without God. That is why they are all rooted in pride. Pride is the vice of putting yourself at the center of things, in God's place, choosing your own way to happiness and believing that any goodness or happiness you have is due to your own power and merit.[23] All the capital vices manifest pride in this way. They are do-it-yourself ways of trying to find fulfillment, rather than dependence-on-God ways of orienting our lives. A prideful disposition says, in effect, "I will decide on what happiness is for me, and I will provide it for myself."

In the medieval depiction of the vices found in the opening pages of this book, Adam and Eve stand at the base of a tree, reaching out for the serpent's proffered fruit. The tree grows up from its prideful roots and then branches out into further limbs of vice. The seven capital vices are the main branches of the tree — they are the first and main offshoots of pride, the original list's eighth member, now taken to be the source of the rest. Each capital vice in turn produces other vices that are depicted as "fruit" or further "offshoots" growing out from the seven main branches.

Cassian first used the tree metaphor, listing offspring vices for each of the capital vices in *Conferences*, Book V, and Gregory canonized the idea of pride as the source of the other capital vices — though with a battle metaphor instead of the organic model of sin — in his *Moralia in Iob*. Aquinas adopts Gregory's lists in his *Summa theologiae* and his *Disputed Questions on Evil* to instruct his readers about the characteristic network of sinful symptoms stemming from all the main vices. Vainglory's particular bitter "fruits" traditionally included *boasting,* which means exaggerating your good qualities, and *hypocrisy,* which means pretending to have good qualities that you don't actually have so that others will think well of you.

Another offspring vice of vainglory — and my personal favorite — is called *presumption of novelties,* a peculiar medieval name for the familiar phenomenon of using, having, or doing the latest and greatest, new and improved, unique and original thing to produce amazement in one's audience and thereby attract (positive) attention to oneself. Consider the example of the iPhone. The ad copy reads, "Unrealized until now. Indispensable from now on. A chip with 64-bit architecture. A fingerprint identity sensor. A better, faster camera. And an operating system built specifically for 64-bit. Any one of these features in a Smartphone would make it ahead of its time. . . . The iPhone 5 is precision crafted down to the micron. And it's evident throughout. The beautiful aluminum housing. The sleekness of metal and glass. Sapphire crystal in the Home button. And more sapphire crystal protecting the iSight camera. Design and construction of this level is unmatched. As a result, iPhone 5 looks and feels unbelievably thin and light. And it's available in three elegant expressions: gold, silver, and space gray." All those features sounded amazing and new when I wrote this, but since that time, several more versions have arrived on the market, all newer and more wondrous still. The advertising genius of Apple and many other companies capitalizes on our desire for sensational and novel gadgets because of the magnetic power of the "new" to draw our attention. As any kid on the school bus knows, anything that is the newest toy or electronic device is a sure-fire attention-getter, and the same goes for adults when it comes to original fashions, concept cars, and the "latest model" of anything else. This goes to show that although there are four other offspring vices of vainglory, if you specialize in presumption of novelties, you probably won't need them. (But in case you're curious, I'll explain the remaining four — obstinacy, discord, contention, and disobedience — in Chapter Four.)

Vainglory's first two offspring vices — boasting and hypocrisy — are familiar and perennial moral problems. Where would the Gastons of this world and the Pharisees among us be without them? But "the presumption of novelties" is also an indispensable concept for analyzing and evaluating our own culture, saturated as it is with advertising, including the self-advertising potential of social networking tools. Thanks to YouTube, you can wow an audience with manifold and marvelous oddities with the mere click of a mouse. Being vainglorious has never been easier.

The traditional tree of vices portrays the offshoot or offspring vices as the morally poisonous fruit of a life devoted to putting something besides God first in our lives. Are these symptoms of vainglory really so bad? Sometimes, and sometimes not. Like the seven capital vices, their forty-nine offspring vices (seven offspring for each vice)[24] are not necessarily singled out because they are particularly pernicious traits in themselves; some are (hatred of God, callousness, and cruelty), and some are not (talkativeness, procrastination, gossip). Rather, they identify the typical marks of a life devoted to substituting some created good for God. To put it in Augustine's words, "My sin consisted in this, that I looked for pleasure, beauty, and truth not in God but in myself and in his other creatures, and the search led me instead to pain, confusion, and error."[25] You can do this with wealth, pretending that having enough stuff will give you self-sufficiency and the security you really need; or you can do this with sexual pleasure or the pleasures of eating and drinking, pretending such pleasures will satisfy your desire for love or your desire for your emptiness to be filled, and so on. Material possessions and security and pleasure are certainly good things. But our desire for them becomes excessive and corrupting when we forget that they are *only* created goods and not ultimate ones. Only God, the source of all created goodness, can have first place in our hearts. The good gifts of God are meant not to claim our ultimate loyalty but to turn our hearts to their Giver in gratitude.[26]

In Augustine's own memorable example, falling prey to a capital vice is like being a woman whose beloved proposes to her. A typical story, except for this twist: after he shows her the engagement ring, her delight in the ring he offers causes her to forget all about him. She doesn't even hear his proposal, much less think to answer it. Can you imagine her taking the ring and walking away without another thought for anything but a piece of beautiful jewelry? She has made a lamentably tragic mistake about what the ring *is*. Her fiancé's gift is not meant to be appreciated merely as a lovely diamond. It's meant to signify his undying love for her and to bind them together in a lifelong relationship. The ring is not just a ring; it is a sign of their love. Accepting it is to accept that gift of love and to return it. The ring, like all good things, is not an object that can be comprehended or held in our possession without essential reference to the one who gave it to us and our relationship to him.[27] And if Augustine is right that only God himself can fulfill our deepest longings, this attempt to substitute love of created goods for the Creator's love is a mistake that also dooms us to dissatisfaction.

Vainglory bears all the hallmarks of a capital vice. It's a disposition — a pattern of thoughts, feelings, and behaviors — that results from putting a happiness-like good at the center of our lives and seeking it without attention to the ways in which that goodness could bring us into closer relationship with God. The good in this case — the engagement ring — is what the tradition calls "glory," a good that is at the heart of human social life and measures of self-worth. Recognizing and receiving it as a gift can deepen our relationship with God. But that gift goes terribly wrong, as we've seen, when we obsess over the gift and go blind to the giver.

When are we mostly likely to make this mistake? According to the tradition, we are most vulnerable when pride and fear cloud our vision and wreak havoc on our desires. Each of these roots produces a vainglorious response in which we unduly seek attention for either a "glory worthy" or a "glory needy" self. St. Augustine gives us a self-portrait of both forms. We'll explore his story in the next chapter.

CHAPTER 3

VAINGLORY'S ROOTS: PRIDE AND FEAR

*To please God . . . to be a real ingredient in the divine happiness
. . . to be loved by God, not merely pitied, but delighted in as an
artist delights in his work or a {parent} in a {child} — it seems
impossible, a weight or burden of glory which our thoughts can
hardly sustain.*

C. S. Lewis, *The Weight of Glory*

THE BEST "VAINGLORY stories" in this chapter are about monks peeling
onions and a teenager stealing pears. They are stories that illustrate two
different roots of vainglory: pride and fear. The Christian tradition had a
lot to say about vainglory's relationship to pride. That's understandable,
since vainglory easily gets tangled up with pride both in theory and in
practice, and it is often difficult to see how the two vices could be distinct.
There's more to the story of vainglory than its prideful roots, however,
so I want to add to the tradition by also linking vainglory to fear. Our
vulnerabilities — just as much as our pride — can drive us to desperate
measures to get glory, even when this turns out to be self-defeating.

Augustine writes his life story as a confession of sin and faith, with
vainglory a bold golden thread woven through his narrative. Moreover,
events in Augustine's life illustrate both the prideful and the fearful roots
of that vainglory and so illuminate its contradictory sources in our lives,
too. After I examine vainglory's "roots and fruits" and the virtue opposed
to it, we'll look to Augustine again to discover its remedies — or, more
modestly, some "practices of resistance" against it.

Prideful Vainglory: Glory-*Worthy* Selves

In the Christian tradition, the link between pride and vainglory is very strong — so strong, in fact, that the two vices often get confused and are typically conflated under the single name of pride. Thus, as we saw in the movie *Se7en,* contemporary lists of the seven deadly sins include pride, but hardly anyone knows what vainglory is anymore. If anything, people use the word "vain" or "vanity" today to mean being conceited or puffed up about yourself (usually in an unjustified way) — roughly speaking, it's a form of pride equivalent to having an inflated sense of your worth or importance.

Thanks in large part to Augustine's and Gregory's influence, the Christian tradition took pride to be the root of all sin. In the Middle Ages, Cassian's "root" metaphor turned visual: artists depicted the vices (and virtues) as trees in illuminated manuscripts.[1] The tree of seven vices was rooted in pride, while the tree of seven virtues was rooted in humility.[2] The other vices (or virtues) branched off the main trunk, with each tree nourished from its root. Translated into practice, this meant there was a sense in which anything sinful ultimately is fruit born of a prideful pattern of playing God, seeking what *we* think is good rather than submitting to God's view. But despite the fact that all sin exhibits this prideful pattern, vainglory and pride were still distinguished as separate vices. Pride was the root of all; vainglory was the first main branch on the tree. The difference, roughly, is that pride is about position and power, and vainglory is about attention and acknowledgment.

Aquinas articulated the distinction between pride and vainglory in the following way. Pride is the inordinate desire for excellence, where "to excel" indicates being better than or superior to someone in some way. "I excel over you" means "I'm better than you" with respect to some good, position, or achievement. So pride is really about the *superiority* of one's goodness. Vainglory, on the other hand, is a disordered desire for the *display* of one's goodness.[3] Put simply, the prideful person desires to be greater than others, whether others recognize this or not, while the vainglorious person wishes to attract others' notice and applause, whether she is better than them or not. Aquinas notes, however, the way the two can work together to generate a vicious circle. The prideful person desires to be superior in goodness to others. Superior goodness naturally attracts attention and approval. But then having more glory than others becomes an additional way in which the prideful person excels over others, and this draws additional notice, and so on. Take a pre-eminent athlete or politician whose achievements make him desirable to follow on Twitter. An impressive following on Twitter adds to his superior status, which in turn increases his celebrity, and publicity for his celebrity status draws even more followers, and so on.

Pride-vainglory hybrid cases like this are typical, even if the two vices can also be distinguished. Interestingly, however, the hybrid case may count as a less developed case of pride. Consider the example of people who are both prideful and vainglorious, like the flag-waving Texas Longhorns fans on a poster proclaiming "PRIDE: Also Bigger in Texas." Such a fan thinks himself (and his team) superior to the rest of us, but he also wants us to recognize that fact and acknowledge it — hence the really big flags and the really loud cheering. Like the character of Scar in *The Lion King* or the Evil Queen before her mirror in *Snow White,* this sort of person wants to be the best *and* wants that superiority to be evident to and duly acknowledged by all. This person wants both excellence *and* its recognition. Something is missing if others don't notice and applaud his greatness.

Compare this sort of person with someone who is prideful but *not* vainglorious. This "purely prideful" person feels far superior to the rest of us — so far superior, in fact, that our opinion of him, our attention and acclamation, mean pathetically little to him. The supremely prideful person might even think it is beneath him to care what others think at all. Their opinions are not worth having. In one Calvin and Hobbes cartoon, older kids mock Calvin for trying to make "snow art" on a warm winter day. Hobbes scornfully labels them "Philistines on the sidewalk." Calvin smirks and agrees: "Genius is never understood in its own time." On the more serious side, the aloof Athenian gentlemen of Aristotle's *Nicomachean Ethics* or Nietzsche's *übermensch* remind us that self-sufficiency, often accompanied by a condescending attitude toward the opinions of the masses, is an essential feature of what makes the prideful person superior: he has risen above needing anything at all from others, even their acknowledgment of his superiority.

On the other hand, we can also construct a case in which vainglorious

43

desires occur *without* prideful motives. Imagine someone who is not particularly interested in putting forth the effort to attain real superiority, nor does she even wish for it. She is happy to be famous for faked goods or pseudo-status, as long as her name stays on everyone's lips. This person doesn't care if her books are of genuinely superior literary value; she just wants them on the bestseller lists. On a larger scale, this is how most marketing works: the advertisers want consumers to find a product appealing, whether that appearance reflects any real value or not. Companies know that people will pay more for a product with attractive packaging than for one without, even if the stuff inside the two boxes is exactly the same. On a more mundane level, recall the popularity games of your middle-school years. Exactly what were the popular people popular *for*? I'm not sure any of us knew then, and I'm pretty sure it didn't matter. In this form of vainglory, people of all ages are consumed only by the desire to get others' attention, to be noticed and approved of by their peer group. This reliance on social approval drives slavish adherence to the canons of "cool," and not only by middle-school students. Especially for those whose sense of self-worth is grounded in the acknowledgment and approval of others, vainglory — rather than pride — is the pressing moral temptation.

Confessions of Prideful Vainglory

St. Augustine, in his *Confessions,* often describes his motives in terms of the hybrid case: prideful vainglory. Under the rubric of the three disordered loves of 1 John 2:16 — "the lust of the flesh, and the lust of the eyes, and the pride of life" (KJV) — he describes his struggle with human praise and vainglory as a case of the last of the three: "the pride of life." Augustine's prideful motives for vainglory are most apparent in his intellectual pursuits, including his education, his career as a professional rhetorician, and, later in life, his preaching. Early in his *Confessions* he links his slavishness to human opinion to a prideful sense of superiority:

> My studies which were deemed respectable had the objective of leading me to distinction as an advocate in the lawcourts, where one's reputation is high in proportion to one's success in deceiving people. . . . I was already

at the top of my class in the rhetor's school, and was pleased with myself for my success and was inflated with conceit. . . . I wanted to distinguish myself as an orator for a damnable and conceited purpose, namely, delight in human vanity.[4]

At this early point in his life, Augustine was concerned with his reputation as a top scholar and an orator. He wanted to be the best, superior at a good thing, but vainglory was his aim, and he describes himself as pleased by the attention his success brought. Augustine got a rush when others acknowledged that he was the best; it made him feel successful, loved, and important (and it assured him of his father's approval as well).

After his years as a student, Augustine became a professional rhetorician. He writes of himself,

Publicly I was a teacher of the liberal arts; privately I professed a false religion — in the former role, I was arrogant, in the latter role, I was superstitious, and in everything, I was vain. . . . We pursued the empty glory of popularity, ambitious for the applause of the audience at the theatre when entering verse competitions to win a garland of mere grass.[5]

To have won the contest with the most eloquent verse was one accomplishment. But the related accomplishment — no less important — was winning the applause that came with it. Which vice was the cause of which? His pursuit of glory is the main expression of his prideful attempts to use human approval to create happiness for himself. But the desire for glory also drives his desire to outdo his competitors. One gets the sense from Augustine that his superiority would have been less satisfying without the public approval that it brought with it. His story shows how the layers of sin can multiply quickly.

After his conversion, Augustine retired from his position as a teacher of rhetoric, laying aside his profession with its vainglorious purposes. But even then we find him confessing to the residual taint of pride in his written works: "The books I [first] wrote . . . were indeed now written at Your service, Lord. . . . But they still breathed the spirit of the school of pride, as if they were at the last gasp."[6]

Augustine's life shows that prideful vainglory is a common and persistent moral problem. And you don't have to be a professional rhetorician to have it. Designating pride as the root of vainglory seems right in many cases, cases in which people not only think of themselves as superior to others, but revel in putting that superiority on parade for others to see. Think of breakaway dunks in the NBA, ostentatious cars and jewelry among the rich, people who are happy to dominate a conversation talking only about the endless drama of their own lives, the rock star who dazzles with a sizzling guitar solo onstage, the neighbors who out-decorate each other each season like they're going to be featured on the cover of *House Beautiful,* the pastors who make sure you know how much larger their congregations are than those in the churches down the street. These folks are not only vainglorious. They think they have "glory-worthy" goods. Their audiences *ought* to admire them for what they have or what they've done, and they therefore put their superiority on display to win the admiration they so desire and believe they deserve.

Even though I cannot dunk and my home is anything but perfectly decorated, Cassian says I might still have to double-check myself for this form of vainglory. Why? Because there's a Christian version of prideful vainglory, too. Listen to Cassian describe the problem in his own monastic community:

> Even in solitude vainglory does not cease to follow the person who, because of vanity, has fled the company of every mortal; the more someone seeks to avoid the whole world, the more hotly it pursues him. Vainglory attempts to puff up one person because he is especially patient in his toil and labor; another because he is very prompt to obey; still another because he exceeds his fellows in humility. . . . Nor does this malady seek to hurt anyone except by way of his virtues, putting out dangerous stumbling blocks precisely where the rewards of life are gained. . . . [Vainglory] wages its assault on us in the very pride of victory over other vices.[7]

Similarly, scholar David Brakke notes, "The monk's battle against vainglory is particularly difficult, for whatever measure the monk uses against it, if successful, can become an occasion for renewed vainglory."[8]

For every step toward superior virtue, wisdom, and spiritual maturity, we face the possibility of desiring that our spiritual status be noticed: "See my great virtue?" We can take pride in our virtue, and we can excessively desire that it be acknowledged, even to the point of silently applauding ourselves. The human capacity for self-consciousness can become a double-edged sword, as we picture the positive reception our spiritual achievements could win for us in the Christian community.

Cassian's memorable image for the devil's power to trap us in vice precisely because of our excellence in virtue is an onion. He writes, "The elders well describe the nature of this malady as similar to an onion or to those bulbs that, when one skin is peeled off, are seen to have another, and as often as they are stripped they are found to be covered."[9] For every gain you make against vainglory, another temptation to it rises. For every layer you peel off, another layer of the same vice can appear. It is layers of the same stuff all the way down.

Keeping Cassian's metaphor in mind, I find it interesting to observe the mature Augustine still struggling with prideful vainglory at the end of his life, during his tenure as Bishop of Hippo, and being vexed that he can't seem to escape the problem. In Book X of the *Confessions* he writes,

> But the word proceeding out of the mouth and the actions which become known to people contain a most hazardous temptation in the love of praise. This likes to gather and beg for support to bolster a kind of private superiority. This is a temptation to me even when I reject it, because of the very fact that I am rejecting it. Often the contempt of vainglory becomes a source of even more vainglory. For vainglory is not being scorned when the contempt of it is something one is proud of.[10]

When pride and vainglory mix, the combination is truly toxic. At the end of his life, Augustine was still peeling the onion and weeping at what he found within.

Fearful Vainglory

Prideful vainglory — the sinful pattern of people who show off their glory-worthy selves — has historically enjoyed a place in the limelight, but another form of vainglory deserves mention, too. This is vainglory's fearful version. The "fearfully vainglorious" are people who are "glory needy" for precisely the opposite reason assumed by the "glory-worthy" prideful: the "glory needy" think they don't have much goodness at all, and they don't want *that* inferiority to be shown or known.

This second sort of vainglorious concern with self-presentation is rooted in a fearful, insecure sense of one's worth rather than a prideful, inflated sense of superiority. The fearful want attention and approval, too, but their constant concern is to keep up appearances and make sure no one sees what lies behind those appearances. The positive public image they present is for a surface self that is paper-thin. Maintaining a mask for others is fundamentally a self-protective maneuver executed when you fear an audience and its power to reject you. The recent plastic-surgery boom is not driven by people who already appreciate the beauty of their own bodies and simply seek minor repairs. The industry thrives on self-loathing, bad body image, and feelings of painful inadequacy. Vainglory is, in cases of fear, not a show-off vice for excellence, but a cover-up maneuver for its acutely felt absence. Likewise, we use our cars and clothing and career credentials to craft images of ourselves we wish to promote and project to others, while keeping much about ourselves carefully hidden from view. The projected image — whether false, selectively true, or just tastefully embellished — is meant simultaneously to keep others from seeing our imperfect and less impressive true selves and to cull recognition and approval for the false fronts we display instead.

In St. Augustine's life, vainglory's fearful form is found right alongside its prideful form. The most well-known example from the *Confessions* is Augustine's story about stealing pears with his teenage friends. In this episode, Augustine's vainglory arises as much from fear of shame and a need to keep up appearances as from pride. Pondering his motives for the theft — pride among them — Augustine admits that fear of social disapproval played a significant role:

> Why then did I derive pleasure from an act I would not have done on my own? . . . But alone I would not have done it, could not have conceivably done it by myself. . . . Friendship can be a dangerous enemy. . . . As soon as the words are spoken, "Let us go and do it," one is ashamed not to be shameless.[11]

Augustine frames Book II with this confession: "[I was] ambitious to win human approval." He longed "to love and be loved" — a theme that resounds throughout the book. In a parallel passage Augustine recounts the lengths to which he was driven by desire for the attention and approval of his friends. His use of the phrase "ashamed to be less shameless" reveals that he found himself driven to vainglory by fear at this stage of his life:

> [I] rushed on headlong with such blindness that, among my friends, I was ashamed to be less shameless than they, when I heard them boasting of their disgraceful exploits — yes, and glorying all the more the worse their baseness was. What is worse, I took pleasure in such exploits, not for the pleasure's sake only but mostly for praise. . . . I pretended to be worse than I was, in order that I might not go lacking for praise. And when in anything I had not sinned as the worst ones in the group, I would still say that I had done what I had not done, in order not to appear contemptible because I was more innocent than they; and not to drop in their esteem because I was more chaste.[12]

This is fourth-century locker room talk. Augustine's friendships at this early stage of his life were marked by lies told to win his friends' admiration and acceptance as "one of the guys."

Augustine's desperation to get attention led him to false friendships. Needing to be known and loved, he found that his vainglorious exploits and pretenses for his peers created distance rather than bringing the sort of acceptance he truly desired. The acknowledgment he did win from his friends was, at this stage of his life, fragile and shallow and conditional on portraying himself as someone he was not.

In his career, too, much of what drove Augustine to seek excellence as a student, and later as a professional rhetorician, was his preoccupation with others' good opinion, in addition to the prideful vanity we heard him confess earlier. He found himself driven by a kind of heedless neediness, despite his admission that human opinion is fickle and not worth having.[13] You can almost hear Augustine's yearning in his description of Hierus, an orator in Rome:

> I had never set eyes on him, but I loved the man for his renown as a person of high culture, because I had heard some words of his quoted that gave me

pleasure. But I loved him above all because others thought him delightful; they praised him to the skies, astonished that a Syrian previously educated in Greek eloquence could later become an admirable orator in Latin as well, and be extremely knowledgeable in the study of philosophical questions. . . . Hence it comes about that a person who is praised comes to be loved.[14]

That is Augustine's strategy in a nutshell — to win praise and glory, because he needed to feel loved. His vulnerability to others' approval as an aspiring rhetorician is evident in his comparison of himself to Hierus:

> That orator was of the type which I so loved that I wanted to be like him. . . . How do I know and how can I be sure in making confession before you that my love for him was aroused by the regard of those praising him rather than by the actual achievements which evoked their praise? If, far from praising him, they had vilified him, and had given a critical and scornful account of his work, my interest would not have been kindled and aroused. Certainly the actual facts would have been no different, nor the man himself. The only alteration would have been in the feeling conveyed by the speakers [about him]. . . . It was important to me whether my discourse and my studies were becoming known to the man. If they met with his approbation, I would have been vastly excited. But if he disapproved, my heart, being vain and void of the solidity you, [O God,] impart, would have been hurt.[15]

Augustine's main concern, as he relates it, was not with Hierus or his work or his worthiness of public approval. Augustine wanted not so much to *be* like Hierus, but to be *popular and celebrated* like Hierus. His main concern was that he be known and loved, not what he was known and loved *for*.

Given these aims, it is not surprising that Augustine notes over and over that most of the people in his profession would say anything — even tell lies — to win applause. He recounts a time when he was preparing a speech in praise of the emperor: "In the course of it," he confesses, "I would tell numerous lies and for my mendacity would win the good opinion of people who knew it to be untrue." When your audience must be pleased, image is everything. As he lied to win friends, so he lied because professional eloquence demanded it; he became a self-described "salesman of words in the markets of rhetoric,"[16] though his discomfort with this role increased as he drew closer to his conversion. His favorite line to describe those in his profession is Psalm 4:3: "They loved vanity and sought after a lie." For those whose fragile egos depend on attention and approval, vainglory becomes a way of life essential to personal and professional success.

In these examples from Augustine's life, and no doubt many we could recount from our own, fear of rejection and excessive dependence on the acknowledgment and affirmation of others are motives for vainglory at least as strong as an inflated sense of one's goodness. Augustine's vain-glory stories from his *Confessions* reveal that anxiety over how we appear to others can drive us just as easily to habitually untruthful self-display. His boastful exaggerations of his exploits might be rooted in pride, but a "glory-needy" self may also move us to do almost anything to secure the approving attention of others, with a deep sense of inadequacy lying close behind our need for recognition and constant stroking.

Fearful Vainglory and the Illusion of Being Loved

Augustine's story also shows us that in cases of fearful vainglory, the temp-tation to falsity and fakery is stronger than in the prideful cases. William Ian Miller, in his book *Faking It,* notes that we live in a "world of posing and shams, anxieties of exposure, and a fear that the 'genuine' may be just another sham whose cover is too tough to be blown."[17] Excessive desire for the attention and approval of others tempts us to put on whatever face will please and to discard truthfulness when it does not serve this overriding end. Hypocrisy conveniently conceals our failure to measure up to socially sanctioned standards; it is driven by our desire to have others' approval even when we don't deserve it — or at least prevent their disapproval.

Unlike boasting and presumption of novelties, and like hypocrisy, vainglory's last four offspring vices — obstinacy, discordancy, conten-tiousness, and disobedience — seem symptomatic of fear and can easily be read as defensive measures that prevent us from appearing in a bad light before others. For example, we obstinately refuse to concede an argument even when we know we're wrong because to admit this would be to lose face. Or we create discord by trying not to look bad in the eyes of others (or even in our own). Or we're contentious and disobedient because we want to convince the doubters watching that we're the sort of person no one can boss around. Our public posturing betrays our anxious hearts in sometimes surprising ways.

Vainglory's fearful form has a distinctive bent toward falsity, hiddenness, staging, and embellishment. Why? This form of vainglory aims, paradoxically, at a self-display designed to *block* a truthful manifestation of ourselves in which we have no confidence. When we are vainglorious, much about us will be widely broadcast, but this is not to say that as persons we will be truly known.

When I first introduced the concept of glory, I noted that human life is properly and best lived in community. We are social creatures, made for fellowship. We flourish in loving friendships. This sort of love requires that we be acknowledged and accepted for who we truly are, not for who we pretend to be or for the appearances we so carefully maintain as masks of acceptability. Real love cannot be blind. To be loved, we must be known. But maintaining our fantastical images and carefully crafted illusions requires deceit and distance from others; our tactics by their nature block truth and thwart intimacy. When we are dominated by fearful vainglory, we focus on an outward presentation of self that others will find winsome, but this wins us acceptance only for a false self. Fearful vainglory makes it impossible for others to know and love us.

It is no accident, then, that Augustine's best experiences of friendship were in Ostia after his conversion, when he was away from the crowds. When he abandoned his career as a rhetorician, he also abandoned a life of falsity and morally corrupting friendships for a life devoted to truth-seeking and true relationships of love. As Augustine discovered the hard way, friendship required sharing himself with another. This fundamental disposition to self-disclosure is opposed to vainglory's false imitation of it. "[All] fame seems to offer," writes Craig Nakken, "is the illusion of being loved."[18] Vainglory's fearful form ironically prompts us to display ourselves, but only in order to conceal ourselves; in its grip, we communicate in ways that block communion. Glory-seeking of this disordered sort thwarts the very sort of acknowledgment and affirmation we need to flourish.

The tradition spent ample energy concerned with pride as a source of sin. Perhaps that's because Cassian and Aquinas assumed their audiences were prone to desire superiority, living as they did in hierarchical communities, or prone to take credit for their own spiritual achievements, given their daily routines of significant spiritual effort. In any case, one problem arises from thinking of yourself as having glory-worthy goods. We've added to traditional accounts another side of the story of the self, the glory-needy side. Those who can't overachieve and draw attention to themselves that way can at least cull some approval with carefully constructed appearances and other defensive maneuvers. However, vainglory, whether rooted in pride or fear, is a self-destructive way to reach for fulfillment.

CHAPTER 4

HONESTY REQUIRED:
HYPOCRISY AND HABITUATION

Hypocrisy is a tribute that vice pays to virtue.

François de la Rochefoucauld

IF YOU HAVE a shallow, less self-aware, and more immature form of vain-glory — like Lady Gaga's appearance-oriented, shock-and-awe glamour — you typically seek glory for superficial goods or in superficial ways, with some form of fakery a likely and appealing strategy. If you have a spiritual, more self-aware form of vainglory — like the Desert Fathers — you're likely to be someone who's morally mature enough to have gotten over the more obvious and crass forms of attention-seeking, but you might nevertheless find yourself more and more preoccupied with the attention and approval others give you for your genuinely glory-worthy qualities.

The skeptical among us might wonder if Lady Gaga is commendable for brassily admitting her desire for fame, while the Desert Fathers sus-piciously flirt with false humility or hypocrisy when they denigrate their own progress in virtue. Truthfulness and falsity come to light as recurring moral concerns across the range of vainglory's shallow and spiritual guises. We need to think more carefully about when and why truthfulness in self-presentation might count as a good thing and the variety of ways in which vainglory distorts and disorders it.

The tradition offers us some cues on this topic in the form of a list of offspring vices assigned to vainglory: boasting, hypocrisy, presumption of novelties, obstinacy, contention, discord, and disobedience. Most of these disordered dispositions involve modes of self-presentation that privilege posturing and reputation-building at the expense of truthfulness. When image is everything, truthfulness is often the first sacrifice on the altar of reputation. For beginners in virtue, the specter of hypocrisy raises a special worry. As we try to acquire virtues, we will likely have had to practice actions that are more aspirational (to act *as if* we had a virtue) than actual reflections of our current character. Our behavior signals a virtuous state that we have not yet fully developed. Is this, too, false pretense?

In this chapter I'll first lay out vainglory's offspring vices to show how a preoccupation with vainglorious show compromises truthfulness in our self-presentation in both direct and indirect ways, and then I'll argue that a beginner's training in virtue need not shade into hypocrisy. I'll also explore how Aquinas's virtue of "truthfulness" gives us a healthy model of self-presentation that's required to make real learning possible and authentic excellence achievable.

Then, in the next chapter, I'll consider the opposite case: the person of mature virtue. For those who are blessed with great gifts that attract notice, handling renown well is a constant challenge. How can people with notable goodness handle well the glory that comes with it, without being tempted to slide from genuine and outstanding virtue into an empty display? In answer, I will use Aquinas's discussion of magnanimity, the virtue of confidently stretching forward to great achievements, to paint a picture of outstanding excellence that is compatible with both truthfulness and humility.

Vainglory's Offspring Vices

In Chapter Two, we saw that the capital vices get their name from their tendency to make some happiness-like good the source and director of the rest of our thoughts and desires, as a substitute for God's place in our lives. Excessive attachment to this central good then spins off vices which are either the means to that good or the effects of pursuing it above all else.[1] For example, greed's offspring vices include theft and fraud and robbery — all of which are means to acquire more wealth or stuff. Greed also spawns restlessness and callousness toward those in need, vices which are the effects of greed's perpetual escalation of desire and discontentment and its focus on material things as objects that can be controlled and secured for one's own possession. These associations between the capital vices and their offspring are loose tendency relations, useful in spiritual direction as a sort of symptom check. Having the characteristic symptoms does not mean that you have the disease, but their presence makes further testing wise.[2] When it comes to vainglory, the central good in question is the "show" of one's goodness, and its offspring vices offer a typical picture of the lifestyle of a person who has organized her life around social recognition as the ultimate reward.

Aquinas divides vainglory's offspring vices (some of which we have already considered) into two categories. First, he considers the vices by which we *directly* seek glory in a disordered way. These include *boasting,* or exaggerating our good qualities (in word); *hypocrisy,* or pretending to have good qualities we do not actually have to make others think well of us (in deed); and *presumption of novelties,* which, as we've seen, is just a peculiar medieval name for the familiar phenomenon of having the latest and greatest, most original and outrageous thing to produce amazement in our audience and thereby attract attention to ourselves. Think of the kid in the back of the bus who shows up with the newest electronic device, and who happily shows it off to the gaggle of oohing and aahing onlookers who crowd in for a closer look. And the presumption of novelties is surely an indispensable epithet to describe a culture saturated with the marvels of advertising, including the self-marketing potential we have through YouTube, Twitter, Instagram, and Facebook. Psychologically, vainglory that's rooted in pride grows into the direct offspring vices, since they are ways of displaying our good qualities positively and proactively. This set of vices usually requires a more assertive "put-yourself-out-there" stance.

Other offspring vices take a more defensive strategy. Through them, we seek glory *indirectly* by showing ourselves *not* to be inferior to others. This strategy is designed to prevent disapproval or disdain from others, rather than increasing or winning us glory. This category of offspring vices includes *obstinacy, contention, discord,* and *disobedience,* a list we encountered briefly in the last chapter. Though still ways of seeking or getting glory, their reactive, damage-control strategy contrasts with the proactive, more assertive approach of boasting, hypocrisy, and the pre-sumption of novelties. Aquinas arranges these indirect offspring vices in an "inside-out" order. In *obstinacy,* we habitually insist on our own judg-ment or reject that of a better judge, so it concerns our opinions and the way we tend to think. In *discord,* we tend to refuse to agree with those wiser than us, so this vice concerns our will.[3] When our obstinacy and discord — those internal habits of mind and heart — break forth into outward expression, this confrontational conversation is called *contention* or quarreling — vainglory defensively expressed in words. Finally, in *disobedience,* we refuse to carry out the command of someone in authority over us. This last vice extends vainglory's reach out into action, partic-ularly when we fear losing face by seeming inferior to someone who can order us around. If we think of a glorious reputation as a competitive good — the more I have, the less you have — conflict sparks quickly and makes submission or agreement unbearable. Our egos are tied to status and reputation, so submission feels like losing face. And it stings more when others are watching.[4]

Think back to when you were a teenager craving recognition and standing as an adult in your own right. When were you most prone to this series of vices, from obstinacy to disobedience? Probably in battles with your parents — and *especially in interactions taking place in front of others.* If your shameless flirting or smoking at the basketball game provoked a word of warning from your disapproving father, your reaction was likely very different if he confronted you at the game than if he talked to you afterwards at home. There's no way you could show your face at school the next day if you listened meekly to a sermon on your inappropriate behavior from your dad while all your friends were watching. (If you argued with your parents in private, it was likely because you genuinely believed your opinions to be true and superior, or you were angry that you couldn't have your own way.) Because your sense of identity is shaky at that age, and you rely excessively on the opinions of your peers for affirmation, you're likely to be especially volatile in public exchanges where you might feel shamed by giving way to another. Of course, Aquinas is thinking of what goes on among those in a hierarchically arranged religious order, but the dynamics he describes certainly transfer to analogous situations at home, at the workplace, and in many other contexts where people have different levels of social power. The question is, has the teenager in all of us ever grown up and gotten over this?

Even though they may be less obvious expressions of vainglory, the indirect offspring vices describe characteristic ways we try to display ourselves favorably to others — with glory as their aim. Both direct and indirect offspring vices — in different ways — push us toward fakery and falsity, exaggeration and excess. The point for the formation of moral character is that a deeply entrenched habit of vainglory tends to branch out and grow into wider and deeper moral corruption. When others acknowledge and affirm us, this is a significant and legitimate good for us — even something that meets a deeply human need. But that means a distorted pursuit of it is also likely to wreak predictable and increasing damage on our characters over time, damage that will leak out into our own actions and our interactions with others. Since we can be genuinely loved and accepted only by being truthful, the cost of vainglorious untruthfulness is high. Moreover, if, like Cassian, we are trying to be intentional and strategic about our training in Christlikeness, we need to know how and why vainglory makes falsity so tempting. That way, we can prepare ourselves against it.

Fake It until You Make It

Once we are acquainted with vainglory's characteristic offspring vices, it is easy to see them everywhere. Hypocrisy is perhaps the most obvious case. We'll consider it now in connection to worries about truthfulness that arise when habit formation — practicing the virtues — is suspected of being just a mask of virtue instead of the real thing. Can learners ever master virtue without faking it until they make it? And can we ever tell from the outside who the real (not merely self-proclaimed) masters of virtue are?

Hypocrisy, Honor, and High Ideals

William Ian Miller, in his book *Faking It,* offers a contemporary perspective on hypocrisy,[5] even though he does not consider its connections to vainglory or name vainglory explicitly as a vice. Miller's irreverent commentary on the Pharisees' ostentatious displays of virtue in chapter six of Matthew's Gospel shows how many layers of hypocrisy are possible in a common "act" of generosity:

> [In Jesus's account of hypocrisy in the Sermon on the Mount,] it is not the hypocrite's deed but his less than virtuous intention that is faulted. The paupers still get their alms either way. The hypocrite's show of virtue does not come cheap; the less than pious motive of desiring public glory for his pious [alms]giving may even prompt him to give more than if he gave secretly. I doubt paupers want to see this form of hypocrisy driven from the face of the earth. From the paupers' point of view, it may be less psychologically demanding to be an insignificant prop in the giver's pageant designed to impress his social equals. Shows of gratitude may not even be required in the paupers' script; their job is to crowd close and then scramble and fall to fighting amongst themselves for the scattered coins. But to receive from a nonhypocritical almsgiver secretly will exact a more stringent recompense in the form of a convincing show of gratefulness.[6]

We might disagree with Miller's cynical take here, but he does raise the concern that hypocrisy may be an unwitting result of a moral tradition that condemns hypocrisy and vainglory but also commends high moral ideals. Judaism has strict legal codes for behavior and severe strictures for those who transgress the law. A Christian ethic tells us to follow Jesus and put on a character like his — full of faithfulness, goodness, and patience, not to mention perfection in virtue. Either way, we know we can't always live up to what we are supposed to be. This means that for most of our moral lives, we are living in the gap, displaying virtuous behavior with less-than-virtuous motives behind it. Miller's claim has a little sting. Does Christianity specially condemn hypocrisy as vainglorious, while simultaneously putting us in the position of being hypocrites most of our lives? There is something to this charge, and another sense in which it does not stick. In our discussion of how we learn to become virtuous later in this chapter, we will find that this gap can be closed by non-vainglorious strategies which require sincerity and truthfulness, while vainglory necessarily thwarts our progress.

Further complicating the matter, as we saw in Chapter One, the early

Christians voiced distinct suspicions of glory. Thus, commenting on non-Christian, honor-driven cultures, Miller says, "Of course you were in it for honor; what better motive could there be worth owning up to that doesn't sound presumptuous or self-satisfied or hypocritical to allege?"[7] The Christian tradition, Miller claims, made honor- and glory-seeking morally problematic: "Faking different motives than the ones you have becomes necessary only once glorying gets a bad name."[8] In other words, people could happily and openly pursue their own glory — until they were told they were supposed to have virtue but not glory, or God's glory but not their own, as their ultimate aim.

Is Miller right? In the *Nicomachean Ethics,* written several centuries before Christ, Aristotle describes three types of human lives. Some people pursue pleasure as their ultimate aim (the hedonistic life), some people pursue honor (the political life), and others pursue knowledge (the contemplative or philosophical life). In his criticism of the honor-loving life, Aristotle points out that honor is something others give to you. He objects to building your life around honor because it makes the success and goodness of your life principally dependent on others' reaction to you rather than dependent on your own actions and character. Further, he argues that the best honor-seekers desire not merely to be honored, but to be *worthy* of honor: that is, they desire to be good people who are living and acting virtuously.[9] In the end, Aristotle says, the political life (a life engaged in the *polis,* or community) is really devoted to cultivating the moral virtues, for which honor is the appropriate result and reward. So even in a Greek, honor-loving culture, non-Christian philosophers argued against making honor the aim of your life. In fact, for Aristotle, seeking honor without virtue gets things exactly backwards, as if one expected a clean bill of health from one's doctor without ever cultivating any healthy habits. Even the Greek philosophers acknowledged the emptiness of seeking honor and glory as ends, over virtue.

Moreover, even when honor and glory are your ultimate aim, Augustine makes a distinction between "the true way" and "the false way" of seeking to be honored for virtue.[10] Augustine uses these categories to analyze the Romans, who wanted to make their names great, renowned in history as great men. In the true way, you cultivate genuine virtue, anticipating that due honor and glory will follow. But in the false or "deceptive" way, you merely pretend to have virtue whenever this will promote personal gains in glory. According to Augustine, Roman devotion to the true way was gradually corrupted into pursuit of the false way.

Is this only a Christian objection? I would argue that it's not. We can see Augustine's distinction echoed in another argument in Greek culture, this time from Plato's *Republic*. In that dialogue, the character Socrates takes up the challenge to defend the intrinsic value of virtue while leaving its "wages and reputation [aside] for others to praise."[11] The characters in the dialogue consider the cynical view — expressed in the story of Gyges of Lydia — that if you have enough power, you can abandon the pursuit of genuine virtue and live a life of deception and hypocrisy, reaping virtue's reward without all the usual onerous moral effort of really being good. Here's the story: The lowly shepherd Gyges stumbles upon a magical ring that makes him invisible. He then sneaks into the palace, kills the king, seduces the queen, and takes over the kingdom. With the power of the ring, he can maintain a reputation for virtue (while he is visible), and still gain the fruits of vice (while he is invisible). Thus, he devotes his life to the unjust pursuit of power and wealth, while seeming a paragon of virtue. Plato's story articulates a challenge to the worth of being moral from those who would champion hypocrisy (and true vice) as the surer and easier path to happiness. To defend the "true way," Plato weaves an answer to the challenge that takes up the rest of *The Republic*.

So, contrary to Miller's claim, concerns with hypocrisy and "false glory" are not new to Christianity or exclusive to its moral concerns about glory. Greek and Roman cultures had conversations on the subject, independent of Christianity's additional cautions about human glory-seeking. As we've seen from Aquinas and Augustine's analysis, though, an additional problem does arise with the advent of a Christian perspective on glory. Yes, we can pursue glory as an end that is empty because it is not properly related to virtue, and we can pursue glorious virtue by true and false means. What Christianity adds is the problem with making glory our end rather than deferring glory ultimately to God, the source of all goodness. It's not only the virtuous or deceptive manner by which we seek glory or the substitution of glory for virtuous activity as an aim that raises a moral problem; it's also the matter of seeking glory for ourselves at all. Christians distinguished this new form of vainglory and named it a capital vice.

The upshot of the analysis is that there are several forms of vainglorious hypocrisy — some recognizable by everyone, and one unique to Christianity. These are temptations that we can fall into singly or together at once. To return to our opening example from Miller and Jesus' Sermon on the Mount, we can deceptively seek to show ourselves virtuous when we are not — hypocrisy, type one — and then take the glory for our faux virtue and appropriate it all for ourselves, while ostensibly giving God glory through our empty religious rituals — hypocrisy, type two. The onion has many layers.

Hypocrisy and Habit Formation

Hypocrisy is clearly a bad thing, isn't it? If our actions purport to express a virtuous motive, but our true, self-serving, vice-riddled motives lie hidden within, what else is there to say but that this sort of deception is not only vainglorious but immoral, period? But wait: What if blanket condemnations of hypocrisy threaten to taint and complicate the necessary workings of good moral formation? To put the objection in Miller's words, it is fortunate for the Christian tradition that hypocrisy may serve as an unwitting stage of virtue formation:

> If you want to appear virtuous to others (and to yourself, too), you might actually have to do more than entertain a few pious thoughts and paste a perpetual look of pitying concern on your face. You might actually have to do some deeds that qualify as good. And lo, by hook or crook, with the very help of that pasted look, you end up doing good deeds with a proper motive, having fooled yourself into goodness.[12]

Aristotle calls this possible gap between action and motive in moral education the difference between acting *according to* virtue and acting *from* virtue. If, for example, certain children share their toys with friends because their parents have bribed them with candy, they *act* generously, but their generous acts do not stem from a generous *disposition* — in fact, from just the opposite. Only when one acts generously because one has the virtue of generosity and values generosity as a worthy character trait do we have a case of complete integrity and sincerity. Aristotle spoke of this as the pursuit of virtue "for its own sake" rather than as a means to some other end (like glory). He thought of this state of virtuous integrity as the end of a long process of moral development which usually starts far from integrity and internal harmony. When we're initially learning to act according to virtue, our imitation of the virtuous person could even be prompted by any number of sub-par and suspicious motives — fear of punishment, desire for a reward like money or pleasure, fear of shame or dishonor, desire for honor or approval, a sense of duty that teeth-grittingly trumps selfish passion, and so on.[13]

Aristotle notes that along the path of moral formation — or "habituation" — motives for actions develop in stages.[14] Fear of punishment (or desire for a pleasant reward like candy) typically motivates learners at the first and lowest stage. Fear of shame and love of honor motivate practice of virtuous action at the second stage, and love of the goodness of virtue itself comes only at the final and highest stage, after much practice and internalization of the goods intrinsic to that type of activity. To illustrate this process, take the practice of piano playing. Initially a child is plunked down on the piano bench and made to practice scales and songs, with suitable sanctions in place if she resists. So she practices to avoid punishment. With practice, she gradually becomes good enough to know what the music should sound like. At this point, she has already learned to recognize and be ashamed of a shabby performance. Even if she still doesn't love her lessons, she does understand and agree with her teacher's assessment of her performance as well or poorly done; she is learning to associate honor with excellence. If all goes well, as she progresses further and become proficient, she learns finally to value excellence itself over honor: she appreciates a good performance because she enjoys the music and delights in it as good. She now loves playing well for its own sake.

Aristotle is savvy enough about human nature to note that in many cases we need our love of virtue to be supported by external sanctions even well into this final stage. For example, I want to do my job with excellence and integrity, because I appreciate the intrinsic value of the work and take delight in a job done well, but it still helps me do that work better and more consistently if I also get paid and have to undergo regular performance reviews. This suggests that we never finally mature into a "pure motive" stage in this life, a conclusion shared by the Desert Fathers.

Rather, we seek to progress continually past our mixed motives and make more and more headway toward the goal of purely virtuous action.[15]

The Desert Fathers offer a view similar to Aristotle's stages of moral motivation. They recommend combating passions like lust and gluttony with love of honor and fear of shame. When faced with a lustful or gluttonous temptation, the monk should consider, "What would others think if they discovered me doing this? What will happen to my reputation if I indulge in this?"[16] Evagrius explains the principle behind this counsel:

> The demon of vainglory is opposed to the demon of fornication [lust], and it is impossible for them to attack the soul at the same time, since the former promises honors and the latter is the forerunner of dishonor. Therefore, if one of these approaches and presses hard upon you, then fashion within yourself the thoughts of the opposing demon. And if you should be able, as the saying goes, [. . .] knock out one nail with another. . . .[17]

The Desert Fathers note that you cannot wholeheartedly desire a "base" pleasure when you are also concerned that indulging in such a pleasure will bring you dishonor. Your abstention from indulgence in shameful pleasure thus stays in line with that of the virtuous person, while your motivation and integrity remain immature.

Caring about honor over pleasure can take two forms — first, caring only about the honor that others will give you if they notice what you've done (or refrained from doing), and second, caring about being an honorable person. The first is shallower and more vaingloriously tainted than the second. No one thinks that abstaining from pleasure only to make yourself look good to others is a morally mature state. Further, how would you restrain yourself from vice when no one else is looking or will ever find out? These are the sorts of test cases that Plato illustrated in the Ring of Gyges story. The point of having a ring that will make you invisible is to indulge in injustice while at the same time upholding one's reputation for justice. Even in the second case, however, someone who feels shame at wrongdoing and who desires social approval for doing right hasn't yet become someone with mature virtue who cares about her integrity in its own right. In both cases, our moral motivations are out of sync with our overtly virtuous appearance. We're left with a gap between motive and behavior.

The practical question is this: If moral development does progress in stages, as we've just described, how can moral educators properly integrate shame and honor, and approval and disapproval from others, into the process of moral habituation without letting hypocrisy or fakery creep in and vaingloriously corrupt the learner's efforts? Is hypocrisy a necessary stage in progress toward virtue? Or can we distinguish cases of sheer fakery in virtue from cases in which we act virtuously, aspiring to be the good persons we are not yet but wish to become?[18] As Miller's "fake it till you make it" example shows, this concern is pressing because when behavior becomes habitual, we easily "live into" our disguises and personas, good or bad.[19] If we project an image of ourselves long enough, our personas begin to feel like the real deal. Far enough into such a life, it might be difficult for the actor herself to tell what is true, because the lines between the self she consistently displays and her inner self have become blurred.[20] Has she become the self outwardly shown, or is she so deceived or confused about her own motives that she can no longer distinguish the two?[21] What begins as a deception of others becomes self-deception. Our vainglory not only blocks others' knowledge of us; it also obscures our self-knowledge — knowledge required for self-examination and confession, practices essential to spiritual formation.

Hypocrisy and "Putting It On"

N. T. Wright addresses the hypocrisy worry in his book *After You Believe: Why Christian Character Matters.*[22] He is not responding to a non-Christian critic such as Miller. Rather, he is speaking to Christians who criticize the formality and fakery involved in following God's rules for Christ-like living when we don't feel like it. These Christian critics share Miller's concerns about authenticity and sincerity, to the point of preferring that we just confess how messed up our motives are and ask for forgiveness and quit the whole program of hypocritical pretense to holiness.[23] Wright acknowledges the worry: "We often use the phrase 'putting on,' of course, in terms of people pretending to be something they are not. The phrase 'putting it on' is a bit of a sneer. 'You're just putting it on,' we say to someone apparently feigning deep emotion; 'you don't really feel like that.' Our culture, soaked in romanticism and existentialism, is quick to spot and laugh at hypocrisy."[24] But Wright continues by pointing out that it's a mistake to condemn every form of "putting on" as hypocrisy. How else can we understand the apostle Paul when he commands the church to "put on the new self" and to "clothe yourself with Christlikeness," a likeness he sums up in a daunting list of virtues — compassion, kindness, faithfulness, patience, gentleness, and love (e.g., in Colossians 3)? "Acting as if" cannot simply be conflated with hypocrisy; rather, like our reluctant pianist's training, it is a process of moral formation in which we deliberately practice actions that we endorse, hoping that they will eventually feel natural and gradually become part of our character. This is a natural and familiar part of the learning process, not something morally alarming.[25] The end of the process is a moral character that feels like "second nature."[26]

Gregg Ten Elshof makes a similar point in his book on self-deception:

> When I imitate something or someone, I adopt patterns of being that are external to me, foreign, and unnatural. . . . Over time, that which was at first artificial, foreign, and unnatural takes root, and I am transformed. . . . This isn't hypocrisy; we don't act contrary to our impulses in an attempt to fake anyone out. We act contrary to our impulses because we wish to be retrained. We wish to be something other than what we are today.[27]

Notably, he argues, this form of training — "transformation through imitation" — is "unavailable to the hyper-authentic," for if you can never act out of step with your current feelings, you will never be able to discipline the immature desires that are now part of your character.[28] Complete consistency of character, which allows only actions perfectly in step with one's current dispositions and feelings, thoughts and imagination, leaves no room for development and growth.[29]

But here's an additional worry: If teachers, mentors, and pastors offer encouragement for behavior that's imitative and not yet genuine, are they thereby rewarding a lack of virtue with glory? Again, that seems too strong. Encouragement helps the process of imitation and habituation to be successful; sometimes it's even necessary to keep us practicing. The encouragement doesn't have to be untruthful; what's important is that it be offered in such a way that the learner believes she can make further progress. In fact, the existentialist philosopher Søren Kierkegaard (1813-1855) claims that this kind of encouragement is an essential feature of love: that it builds others up precisely by imagining better character in them than they presently have, and "loves them up" into that image.[30] The encourager imitates God, who loves us while we were yet sinners, and yet calls us to holiness.

Help for Hypocrites: Keeping It Real

This virtue-based approach to moral formation has the advantage of being realistic, rather than overly optimistic or overly pessimistic about human nature. It doesn't unreasonably assume that people are capable of perfect moral compliance in their current state, but it also does not assume that their failure to measure up is so fixed that any plan for progress is irrelevant.[31] It acknowledges that moving toward maturity in virtue takes both time and practice. A virtue approach can thus make high moral demands of us ("Be perfect, as your Father is perfect"), while offering us a lifelong program of character development to make progress in meeting those demands. Put in theological terms, sanctification — an arc of increasing holiness — is expected, made possible by the Holy Spirit's work and our cooperation.[32] Thinking about virtue in this developmental way helps us avoid charges of hypocrisy. We're not faking something; we admit that we're genuinely trying to become something we're not yet. And the process isn't doomed to failure; although we need confession for our current moral state, we also *can* develop more Christ-like character.

How then can we distinguish the morally pernicious type of hypocrisy from the salutary process of moral habituation? First, by recognizing that our aims will determine how we self-disclose. The vainglorious hypocrite that Jesus condemns aims to be known and shown as a pious person, even though he doesn't really care about true piety. So he does his best to cover up the disconnect (perhaps even to himself, in self-deception) and to prevent others from correcting it. The true disciple takes the opposite tack. It's painful to expose her fumbling efforts and to own up to the "lack of fit" during the process of becoming virtuous. Her aim is true piety, however, so she has good reason to reveal herself: it's necessary to get the good counsel and correction she needs to make progress toward greater integrity. Let me extend my earlier analogy of the piano. If as a young child I wanted to play a piano piece better, I had to perform it — faltering rhythms, bad fingerings, and all — for my teacher's critical ear. I had to be willing to show her my flaws in order to improve. And improvement was the reason I was taking lessons. If I played a piece too fast or added pedal so my uneven notes or sloppy fingerings would elude her notice, I would hinder my own progress and purposes. (If you're lucky, your teacher will be too careful a listener for those tactics to work very well.) As with moral formation, truthful self-presentation — warts and all — was essential to the process. Unlike the hypocrite, the disciple is truly trying to become the person he projects.[33] The hypocritical person must cover up his failures; but for the disciple, cover-up is self-defeating.

In both habituation and hypocrisy, our outward show lacks inner substance. To distinguish the slow, sometimes painful process of moral formation from hypocritical shams, we'd do well to double-check for truthful self-disclosure. Danger lurks when we are tempted to settle for a sham reputation rather than doing the hard work to make our virtue real. If there is a chasm between our current character, our public performances, and our calling to true and perfect virtue, are we willing to be truthful about it? The truthful virtue-seeker will risk the pain of exposure now to become better in the long run, while the hypocrite settles for the short-term safety of publicly approved appearances.

Being Yourself

As we will see in the next chapter, when Aquinas opposes the vice of vainglory to the virtue of magnanimity, this has the effect of putting emphasis on the *goodness* displayed: Is it great? Worthy of respect, honor, awe, and admiration? Maintaining magnanimity against vainglory is a test of how tenaciously we value genuine goodness or excellence. In Aquinas's discussion of vainglory and the virtue of truthfulness, however, the emphasis is on the *manifestation* of goodness and its match to reality — the accuracy of the display itself. His account of truthfulness gives us a name for the underlying ideal of self-presentation that is both accurate and appropriate. Why do we need such an ideal, and why is it worth naming? Even in a culture that ennobles authentic self-expression, vainglory's offspring vices, especially hypocrisy, speak volumes about how uncomfortable we feel showing others who we really are. We would rather Photoshop enhanced and retouched versions of ourselves for public consumption, whether we want to intimidate the competition or just fit in. Is your reputation for real? This virtue focuses attention on vainglory not in word but in deed.

"Truthfulness" usually brings to mind *saying* true things. But what if it also means *being* truthful in how we present ourselves to others, rather than letting a carefully constructed reputation cover reality? We don't ordinarily think of being truthful as extending beyond words, but Aquinas understands truthfulness as a virtue regarding self-manifestation in verbal *and* non-verbal ways.[34] We can smile at those we despise, cross our arms in disapproval when we are secretly hoping someone will get away with revenge, stand defiantly when we are cringing inside from fear of shame, and whistle our way cheerfully through a job while our stomach tightens in knots of anxiety. We are not always what we profess or pretend outwardly to be. Vainglory is a prime motive for untruthful communication about ourselves, as we've already noted. But it's worth revisiting vainglory's most familiar offspring vices, especially hypocrisy, now with a focus on vainglory's damage to authenticity and integrity in our self-presentation.

Contrary to what you might expect from the name of this virtue *(veritas)*, Aquinas does not want to talk about truth-telling or honesty generally, or limit truthfulness to strictly obligatory contexts (e.g., promise-keeping, witnessing in court). Instead, this virtue is concerned with properly "manifesting to others things that concern yourself" in sometimes subtle but everyday ways. When I'm at a business conference, what does it say about me if I keep conversations strictly work-related, or if I also share stories about my family life? When I speak in front of a group, do I work to stand up straighter and project a level and confident tone? When I see depictions of suffering at a movie theater, do I openly show emotion, or do I keep my feelings inside? When I'm asking for a favor from my superiors at work, do I take a deliberately deferential stance? When I dress for a date, or for work, or for church, what "look" am I aiming for? When I find myself with a judgmental person, do I defend myself by making self-deprecating jokes or over-apologizing, or do I add a little bluster to my response? When I first meet someone new, would I rather be mistaken for being too arrogant and aloof or too warm and affectionate? When I head to the mall, do I dress in clothes that conform to or defy social convention? Or do I signal my allegiance to some subculture by flouting my parents' or my society's standards of decency? What do I say about myself when I make these choices? In other words, the virtue I'm calling "truthfulness" (with Aquinas) is primarily concerned with how we appropriately display ourselves to others, focusing on sincere but socially appropriate self-disclosure. The moral issues here include the ways we disclose ourselves in speech, but aren't limited to instances of verbal self-expression.[35] They concern the integrity (or lack of it) between who you are and the public image you present to others.

In Aquinas's words, the virtue of truthfulness concerns "only that truth where a person, both in life and in speech, shows oneself to be such as one is, and the things that concern one to be not other, and neither greater nor less, than they are."[36] If you are truthful in the way Aquinas is talking about, you will reliably give a true, socially appropriate, and context-sensitive account of yourself that reveals neither too little nor too much. The way we use the terms "integrity" and "sincerity" and even "authenticity"[37] overlap with some, but not all, of the same ground as truthfulness. As will also be shown to be true of magnanimity and humility, truthful presentation of yourself depends on having an accurate assessment of yourself, including a true assessment of your own goodness (or lack thereof) and your desires concerning what you want others to think about you.

We could sketch several character portraits of people who lack truthfulness. Some of us tend toward over-communication. Have you ever exaggerated your righteousness in recounting an argument? Aggrieved and offended, you portrayed yourself as the clear victim in need of redress, when the matter was much more complicated and nuanced. Others of us tend toward under-communication. Have you ever stood silent when it was clear that you were the only dissenter in a strongly opinionated group? You knew you would be attacked if you spoke up, and perhaps treated badly, and so out of fear or to avoid a fuss you let others assume you were in agreement and let the matter pass.

Why might we fall into self-displays that fall short of truthfulness? Not surprisingly, Aquinas comes right back to vainglory when he probes our underlying motive. We also won't be surprised to see him name vainglory's signature offspring vices as classic ways to give a false or misleadingly incomplete representation of ourselves. Along with ordinary cases of lying,[38] his list of vices undercutting the virtue of truthfulness includes *dissimulation* or *hypocrisy*. Hypocrisy, as he means it here, specifically means signifying "by outward signs of deeds or things . . . that which one is not" — something like the opposite of sincerity. Here the focus is on your actions and whether they present you truthfully to others. Are you drinking a wine you find bitter and smoking a cigar you find distasteful just to impress the highbrow company you're with? Are you laughing at vulgar jokes you find offensive to be accepted by the lowbrow company you're with? To simulate is a misuse of signs and cues to pretend to be something you are not, in contrast to the right use of them to genuinely signify what you are.[39] When someone mistakes the rented Mercedes you purr up to the curb in for your own car, do you laughingly clear up the confusion or let him believe what he will? When a co-worker flirts and throws around a little sexual innuendo, do you smile and play it off even though you disapprove and it feels demeaning? Hypocrisy, on this definition, primarily concerns ways of presenting ourselves and, by extension, our goodness to others through expressing ourselves in actions and postures. These physical cues, like words we speak, function as signs deliberately mismatched with what they are meant to signify.

Retouching the Remembered Self

If our audience is not fooled, should we have moral qualms about these familiar genres of miscommunication? Perhaps. Aquinas scholar Josef Pieper warns that repeating these stories out loud or even in our minds sometimes has the power to alter our actual memories. "There is no more insidious way for error to establish itself than by this falsification of the memory through slight retouches, . . . omissions, shifts of accent."[40] If we make retouching the past a habit, we can lose touch with what is real and what is not, even in our own heads. Vainglorious practices can lead to a kind of un-self-detectable "lying to ourselves." This could be motivated by a deep unwillingness to admit something bad about ourselves, out of fear and shame; it could equally well be motivated by blinding narcissistic tendencies — a version of prideful vainglory. Take this example from Jerry Sandusky's trial for forty-five counts of child abuse, reported by *The New York Times:*

> Mr. Sandusky's remarks Tuesday at times resembled a pregame motivational speech, perhaps reflecting his years as a widely admired defensive assistant for Mr. Paterno. Casting himself in the role of an underdog fighting against a conspiracy to find him guilty, Mr. Sandusky mentioned that *Seabiscuit* was one of his favorite movies. He read aloud a letter from a boy who described Mr. Sandusky as a savior for his life and called him Touchdown Jerry. And he emphasized how he brought joy to children through activities like water balloon fights.

Other participants in the trial were skeptical of his self-presentation. The *Times* story continued: "'His statement today was a masterpiece in banal self-delusion, completely untethered from reality and without any acceptance of responsibility,' said Joseph E. McGettigan III, the lead prosecutor. 'It was entirely self-focused, as if he, him, were the victim. It was, in short, ridiculous.' Judge Cleland deemed Mr. Sandusky's statement 'unbelievable.'"[41] The problem, it seems, is that Sandusky himself believed his own selective memory and self-serving spin. Not only his external truthfulness but his internal truthfulness, too, had been eaten away by wanting to appear — not only to others, but to himself — as having goodness that was in no way related to the man he had truthfully become.

The same dangers apply when we repeat exaggerated accounts of our exploits in spiritual matters. As Gregory puts it, "Hypocrites make God's interests subservient to worldly purposes, since by making a show of saintly conduct they seek, not to turn others to God, but to draw to themselves the applause of [others'] approval."[42] In the end, however, we may be fooling ourselves. Who is our religious practice for? Can we be honest before God with our motives if we are not honest with ourselves?

Gregory and Aquinas point to pride as the familiar motive for boastfully untruthful behavior. But, as we've seen in Chapter Three, fearfulness and the desperate need for others' acceptance can be at least as compelling a motive as an overinflated sense of oneself. Vainglory's offspring vices, especially hypocrisy, are simply more symptoms of the same root problem that stands behind the capital vice itself. Whatever our methods, we are using our audience to assuage our longing for acceptance and our "overriding concern for confirmation or security"[43] — even to the point that we, like Cassian's preaching monk, create an approving audience in our own heads. Our need for attention and approval tempts us to discard truthfulness when it's inconvenient and to disregard proper self-disclosure when it does not conveniently serve our vainglorious goals.

When we are controlled by vice in this way, our untruthful communication about ourselves manipulates others in order to promote a certain image of ourselves. We not only deviate from the truth through morally disordered means of communication; we also use those means for a morally disordered end. Whether vainglory takes the form of prideful self-promotion or fearful self-protection, it drives us to display a false front, carefully crafted to please our audience. But friendship and love cannot survive without truthfulness, nor can a healthy view of ourselves. To love me is to *know* me, and to know *me*. Love for each other and for ourselves must be built on a foundation of truthfulness. Vainglory deals it a deadly blow.

CHAPTER 5

MAKING A MOCKERY OF MAGNIFICENT VIRTUE

When God at first made man,
Having a glass of blessings standing by,
Let us (said he) pour on him all we can:
Let the world's riches, which dispersed lie,
Contract into a span.

No sooner is a temple built to God,
but the Devil builds a chapel hard by.

George Herbert

Vainglory and the Virtue of Magnanimity

THE SECOND AREA of concern with truthfulness has to do with a process that moves in exactly the opposite direction of the learner. In the learner's case, he aspires through repeated and honestly deficient outward conformity to authentically become something good that he is not (yet). In the case of the truly mature or magnificently virtuous person, under vainglorious pressure that virtue can degenerate into an empty masquerade. Magnanimity is a virtue that showcases the genuine goodness that vainglory undercuts. Aquinas's examination of it addresses the problem of the person of excellent or exceptional virtue who — as a matter of her position or calling or spiritual gifts — cannot dodge the difficult task of trying to handle glory well.

Glory is defined as the display of *goodness,* but one of vainglory's most striking features is that its attraction to attention so easily slips away from that standard. Aquinas puts it rather bluntly: we can glory vainly in anything we do have and in anything we don't.[1] Vainglory's "have" and "have not" forms reveal two different strains of vainglorious temptation. For those who *have* glory-worthy goods, the temptation is sliding from real striving after virtue into living off their past reputation. So in this section, we'll look at a trio of vices opposed to the virtue of magnanimity to see how Aquinas warns us against this mistake.

Magnanimity: Glory-worthy Greatness

One way we can read Aquinas's different discussions of vainglory is by focusing on different parts of its name. One text emphasizes what's vain; another emphasizes glory. In the text called *Disputed Questions on Evil,* Aquinas treats the capital vices together as a set of seven without the context of the virtues they oppose. There the vainglorious person's false claims to goodness take center stage — it's all about the emptiness or *vanity* of her claims to fame. But in the *Summa theologiae,* where Aquinas frames the ethical life around the virtues, he adds in vices only insofar as they corrupt those particular kinds of goodness. There the story of vainglory begins from a great person's true claims to *glory.* Nowhere is this clearer than when he talks about the virtue of magnanimity.

Magnanimity is a mouthful to pronounce. The Latin word (from *magna anima*) literally means "greatness of heart" or "being great-souled." But this virtue is a stumbling block in more significant ways than its pronunciation, as we will see in a moment. A person with magnanimity is Aquinas's reshaped and rehabilitated version of Aristotle's "great-souled man," a paragon of the virtues.[2] Such paragons have glory-worthy goods — truly monumental and magnificent achievements in virtue. Their extraordinarily good achievements naturally garner extraordinary acclaim. When Jimmy Carter, Nelson Mandela, and Mother Teresa win Nobel Peace Prizes for their goodness, they don't have the option of avoiding the limelight. How do they handle glory well? These are cases of genuine goodness getting glory, the cases of greatest concern in the Christian tradition.

It's striking, however, that Aquinas accepts magnanimity as a virtue at all. He associates four possible vices with magnanimity, instead of the two he usually assigns as possible corruptions of a virtue. And he departs from his style of brief summary to defend magnanimity's claim to virtue against a slew of possible criticisms. It's as if he's highlighting how easily things can go wrong for the magnanimous person.[3] Why does Aquinas labor to include this virtue? And what does he mean to teach us about vainglory by including it?

Aquinas agrees with Augustine and the earlier Christian tradition that glory is properly due ultimately to God. But he disagrees with advice from Cassian and Benedict's rule for monks that one should avoid all occasions for glory. Consider Cassian's counsel: we should "strive utterly to reject as the stuff of boastfulness whatever is not generally accepted and practiced . . . and we must avoid those things that could set us apart from others and that would gain us praise from human beings, as if we were the only ones who could do them."[4] In other words, monks should avoid vainglory by pursuing unexceptional, ordinary lives which attract little or no attention from others.

In stark contrast, Aquinas works to include magnanimity in his ethics, and defines it as stretching oneself to perform great acts of virtue. And he includes it despite the attendant difficulty of virtuously handling the honor and glory that result from those great acts, a difficulty well-documented already among the Desert Fathers. From the days of their exemplar St. Anthony onward, they knew that their lives of radical discipleship brought great renown and attracted pilgrims from all over the world, even though the monks sought a life of solitary prayer. Rather than recommending that we renounce claims to glory, or (heaven forbid) scale back on virtue to avoid glory, Aquinas adopts the following logic: If virtue's natural reward is honor and glory, and greater virtue elicits greater honor and glory, and if God calls us to perfect (i.e., great) virtue, then we'd better confront the task of handling honor and glory well.

Magnanimity: Greatness and Grace

To tackle this task, Aquinas must craft a significant transformation of magnanimity. The magnanimous or great-souled person of Aristotle's *Nicomachean Ethics* is a person who has to handle great honors well because he is a public figure and a person of outstanding virtue. But it is difficult to read Aristotle's description of this exemplary, virtuous person without being struck by what Christians would likely identify as the magnanimous man's obvious pride. His condescending manner, for example, comes from despising the opinions of the general public, whom he deems (correctly, in Aristotle's opinion) unworthy judges of his true worth and greatness. With his slow, regal gait and his few words, he stands above the rush of ordinary life, concerned only with weighty affairs of great import. He aspires to self-sufficiency, and therefore prefers giving to receiving, lest he be dependent on others for anything. The magnanimous man provides a rather sharp contrast to the Christian virtue of humility,[5] which held a central place among Christian virtues: recall that it often served as the root of the tree of virtues, opposite pride, the root of all the vices.[6]

How does Aquinas win over Christian critics of Aristotle's portrait of greatness? His bold move is to ground the magnanimous person's confidence in her ability to act virtuously *by God's grace*. Her confident reaching out toward great acts of virtue and their accomplishment are possible only because they rest on God's power.[7] This is especially true when her virtuous action stretches her human capacities to the limit and draws recognition and respect for her tremendous achievements. The magnanimous person's serenity in the face of such challenge comes from her reliance on God's help to accomplish what is needful for virtue, even if this calls her beyond the reach of her own power and imagination, and even if this inspires scorn or skepticism from other people. Aquinas argues that the magnanimous person often tunes out human opinion polls because her ear is tuned to God's voice, and it is enough for her to hear "Well done, good and faithful servant" from him.[8] When she is unconcerned about how others may perceive and judge her, this arises from her trust that God's love makes her secure, whichever way the wind of human opinion may blow.

Eleonore Stump, in her philosophical treatment of the problem of suffering, paints a portrait of the woman who anoints Jesus' feet (Matt. 26:6-13) as someone whose magnanimously great expression of love shocks and offends her human audience, even as it is publicly affirmed and defended by Jesus. Not only does his standard of her greatness trump the human standards that shame her; it is also crucial for her (and for her human audience) that he express this in a public social setting. Stump stresses that the woman's goodness must be *made known* to her and to her society by Jesus:

Because Jesus honored her, and in that public way, [the woman] will have been shown how to know herself, not by the local community measure that has shamed her, but by a deeper and more important measure that honors her. In the memory of the measure shown to her by Jesus, she will learn the honor of herself, which is a necessary ingredient in her peace.[9]

Stump notes that Jesus' public regard gives the woman a true audience (and simultaneously corrects her human audience). Jesus is someone who, in affirming her in this way, gives her a true measure of what her own self-regard should be like, as a human being created but "a little lower than the angels, and crowned with glory and honor" (Ps. 8:5).

Unlike Aristotle's model, which could not countenance the magnanimity of this anointing woman, Aquinas's model of magnanimity is compatible with the Christian virtue of humility. In his account, the magnanimous person truthfully sees how fully dependent she is on the restoring and enriching power of God, because she recognizes the limits of her own powers of greatness. But her dependence on God will, I think, also make her *less* dependent on her human audience for attention to her greatness and affirmation when she is stretching herself to the full extent of her gifts (with all the risks and pressures that may bring). In this way, the magnanimous person shows us a model of detachment — or, more positively, freedom — in the same way that the generous person shows us detachment or freedom from holding onto money, or thinking of it as something she ultimately owns or is owed.

By reworking magnanimity this way, Aquinas is clearly endorsing Augustine's view of virtue as a quality "which God works in us without our help":[10]

> There is in human beings something great which they possess through the gift of God; and something defective which accrues to them through the weakness of their nature. Accordingly, magnanimity makes them deem themselves worthy of great things in consideration of the gifts they hold from God: thus if their souls are endowed with great virtue, magnanimity makes them tend to perfect works of virtue; and the same is to be said of the use of any other good, such as knowledge or external fortune. On the other hand, humility makes them think little of themselves in consideration of their own deficiency. . . .[11]

The magnanimous person is not a "self-made man" and virtuous over-achiever but an awe-inspiring picture of the power of the Holy Spirit operating in and through an otherwise ordinary human being to enable virtuous acts beyond what he can ask or imagine.[12]

Magnanimity Gone Wrong: Losing Your Grip on Greatness

But with great virtue comes great temptation. It's one thing to respond willingly if you have little or no social standing and you are surprisingly singled out by God to do something great. But if that greatness puts you in the spotlight, it's another task altogether to handle that greatness and glory well then *and* in all the years that follow.

We can mishandle magnanimity by overreaching in at least three ways, vices Aquinas names "presumption,"[13] "ambition,"[14] and "vainglory." (A fourth vice is one of "under-reaching"; named "pusillanimity," magnanimity's opposite is a vice of shrinking back from great acts of virtue for lack of confidence.) Presumption and ambition (both used in a pejorative sense in the Latin) directly concern magnanimity's great acts of virtue and the great honors those acts receive.[15] Great virtue and great honors are indeed good things; but, like vainglory, the vices of presumption and ambition concern disordered desires for them. Either we presumptuously assume more power than we do have (or that God gives us), or we are overly attached to the honor that follows our great acts.

Vainglory, the last of magnanimity's three opposing vices, trails in their wake: it concerns wanting the *renown* that comes from doing great things and being honored for them. For Aquinas, glory is "an effect of honor and praise: because from the fact that someone is praised, or shown any kind of reverence, that person acquires clarity in the knowledge of others."[16] The general idea is that doing great deeds of virtue will win you honor, and, in turn, being honored or shown reverence will bring you renown; it will make your (good) name known far and wide.[17] Aquinas orders his account of the vices to begin with acts of genuinely awe-inspiring virtue and gradually considers the ripple effects of such acts in the responses of others. Vainglory lies on the outer circle, farthest away from the virtuous action itself and closest to others' reactions to it. Juxtaposing vainglory with magnanimous virtue and its natural effects highlights acts of astonishing virtue that naturally garner significant attention.

Imagine Mother Teresa receiving her Nobel Peace Prize. After all the receptions and interviews, an anonymous life in Calcutta might seem incredibly dull by comparison; on the streets she is uncomfortable, unnoticed, a drudge tending to the needs of the poor. Her faithful and virtuous charitable work was tolerable until she was forcibly presented with a more exciting alternative. Now, sitting in her plainly furnished and quiet room, she remembers what it felt like to walk on stage, under the lights, and hear the thunderous applause. She re-imagines the moment, savoring the memory, feeling the power of sharing her message of self-giving love with the world. Won't the ordinary grind of life now leave her a bit impatient and restless? One day she takes a phone call and agrees to another interview, which leads to a few more interviews, a commencement speech or two, and then a spot on the *Today Show.* Soon she is well poised to go on a whirlwind global tour, complete with rallies and media blitzes.

Of course, it's hard to conceive of this change happening quickly to anyone, and it's all but impossible to imagine it happening to a paragon of Christian virtue like Mother Teresa. Which leads me to ask two other questions: What made Mother Teresa so resistant to this temptation? And, on the other hand, how much more imaginable is this scenario if we begin with ordinary people with weaker character and give the process years to develop? Actually, we don't have to imagine this at all. Given the media scrutiny of every policy statement they make, don't even those politicians who begin their careers with integrity and a concern for public service seem like vainglorious accidents just waiting to happen after a term or two in office? How about the insightful and gifted preacher invited to give a sermon at a significant service who finds herself short on ideas and short on time to prepare? Will she strain under the pressure to plagiarize so she can deliver a stirring message commensurate with her audience's expectations of excellence? What about athletes who are tempted to use performance-enhancing drugs as they grow older and slower? On a smaller scale, don't many of us who are well into our careers want to hold onto our titles and the deference of our co-workers long after we are willing to put in the long hours needed to earn respect? Have you ever known someone who was a vibrant and faithful Christian who became more attached to his standing among others at church than actually maintaining a rich relationship with Jesus? It's common to feel the lure of living off a lovely reputation even when the reality behind it has faded. And it's easy to get tired of the extra effort it takes to maintain excellence over the long haul, just as it's hard to admit we're not as good as we used to be.

Aquinas's triplet of associated vices addresses the degeneration of real virtue (or real achievement) into a life of keeping up one's previously glorious appearances. Such is the story of the slide from virtue to vainglory.

When Aquinas talks about virtue, he starts with the goods at stake, explaining what well-ordered desires for them are like. Then he proceeds to deviations and disorders — the various vices. In the case of magnanimity, the goods related to it flow in one direction, from cause to effect: outstandingly good actions are naturally followed by due honor and praise, which in turn are followed by reputation and renown. The vices then follow this same order of goods, now as inordinately desired. So in his order of presentation, Aquinas depicts the history of a typical moral slide.

If we had to summarize the connections that Aquinas intends between magnanimity's three vices of excess, we could say this. The presumptuous person overreaches to do great acts that are above her power, overestimating her abilities out of a desire to be greater than she is.[18] She feels untouchable, unconquerable; in extreme cases her self-assessment shades into the megalomaniacal. Why can't this person step down from power and out of the limelight? Because she is *the best.* She can do anything.

The ambitious person desires too much to receive honor from others. (This may or may not lead him to overreach his capacities presumptuously.) The star player learns to expect the awe of his opponents and deferential treatment from the referees. He learns to expect respect as a matter of course, even in arenas in which his greatness is irrelevant. His prowess on the basketball court means that the President should invite him to the White House to shake his hand. If he is not awarded due respect, he feels slighted.

In general, the connection between these two vices, while not necessary, does seem fairly natural (and in both directions). The excessive love of honor tends to prompt presumptively ill-conceived attempts at great acts: for example, coming out of retirement to face a younger opponent in order to hold onto one's athletic title; hastily publishing a new but sloppier book because one has received prior acclaim for one's scholarship and the critics eagerly expect more. Overreaching for greatness in actions likewise engenders excessive expectations of honor for them. Think of the overachieving student who spends four years of high school trying to be named valedictorian, or the workaholic who expects his efforts to win him the company's Employee of the Year award. It's easy to see how these cases can degenerate one step further. If the magnanimous person slides from seeking something of genuine value (excellent achievement or virtue), to becoming enamored of the respect he receives from having that good, to becoming addicted to his audience's attention and approval ratings, whether he has the goods that warrant them or not, he's landed in vainglory.

What distinguishes this last stage? Presumption and ambition still retain *some* link to honor-worthy acts of virtue, since honor itself is more than mere attention — it is a form of respect for something worthy. Vainglory, the last vice in the chain, shows us where we end up when a desire for attention has so fundamentally undercut our value of goods with real worth that we forego them entirely and settle for the outward show. It is one level of corruption to seek to do virtuous actions not so much because we value their goodness but because we desire to receive honor for them. It is a further step away, however, to have the end of the entire enterprise be renown — the maintenance or protection of a reputation that is not (or no longer) supported by actual goodness. In vainglory's most extreme forms, the link between what is good and worthy of glory and the public image that gets attention breaks down altogether. The vainglorious person has sold glorious reality for the appearance of it, and serious achievements for its shallow and superficial imitation.

As Jake Halpern's sought-after professor of television studies illustrated already in Chapter One, a taste of this sort of attention can be highly addictive. In an interview in 2011, the late actor and comedian Robin Williams remarked, "I think celebrity itself is a drug. . . . And now with tweeting and Facebook, it's like cybercrack."[19] Such attention gives us the patina of acceptance and respect, so easily (mis)taken for the real thing because of our great need for it. The presumptuous person's actions are guided by her desire for real greatness, even if she overestimates her power to achieve it on her own, and the ambitious person's actions are directed by her desire for respect, even if this desire is excessively enslaved to human approval. But the vainglorious person lets go of those limits. She is willing to do anything for attention — even fake it.

What Not to Think About

Magnanimity is a virtue that's compatible with Christian humility, but we might say something even stronger than that: magnanimity will count as virtuous only if it is actually combined with humility. How might this look? Humility is often mischaracterized as an unduly low estimation of oneself, a self-deprecating, self-undermining sense of one's own debased status. Robert C. Roberts and W. Jay Wood offer a better definition of this virtue, however, one that highlights what it shares with magnanimity. They describe humility as "an unusually low concern for status coordinated with an intense concern for some . . . good" and a "relative lack of concern to appear excellent to others."[20] This definition could just as well be a definition of virtuous magnanimity, if we focus the emphasis on being so concerned with excellence and its achievement that we are free to boldly attempt great things without regard to failure or disapproval in the eyes of others, and with regard primarily for what is important in God's eyes. In this sense, Mary the mother of God was both humble and magnanimous. Roberts and Wood also give the example of G. E. Moore, a professor of philosophy who would stand back from the lectures he had given the day before and freely criticize them as if they were someone else's views, without any ego on the line. His focus was on the subject matter, not his own appearance as an expert.

What magnanimity and humility share is a preoccupation with the good in view (finding the truth, or the beauty of some great virtuous action) rather than with the self as seen by others. "Status-relevant appearances"[21] are simply on the mental back-burner, if they are in one's awareness at all. In his studies of human enjoyment, psychologist Mihalyi Csikszentmihalyi calls a certain kind of intense engagement in projects or activities that we find intrinsically rewarding a "flow experience." In a flow experience, we are so focused on the activity and absorbed in what we are doing that we "lose a sense of ourselves doing it" and also, sometimes, a sense of time passing.[22] Whether we are reflecting on what God has called us to, or unreflectively engaging wholeheartedly in an activity with "flow," what preoccupies our attention is the good, not the self, not its appearance to others or its status. If we take this point to its biblical limits, the virtues of magnanimity and humility enable us to shrug off both potential shame and potential celebrity, preferring God's work and wisdom to all else. Paul is willing to look foolish compared to the wisdom of the philosophers, and to jettison his Jewish credentials as rubbish, all for the sake of the gospel he is called to preach (1 Cor. 1:18-30; Phil. 3:4-8). If we lose our grip on this sense of what is truly important, attending too much to how we appear to others, then vainglory can begin to gain traction.

Someone from an audience at a conference once asked me how I manage to give public talks on vainglory, complete with applause and adulation, without letting the glory go to my head. For the truly excellent among us, this is a pressing practical matter. But it matters for the rest of us too! The answer in my own case is that when I leave the lecture hall, I go home to my children, who think philosophical expertise and whatever other important things I think I am offering the world through my job are of little or no importance. In their world, my job is distant and insignificant; no failure or success, no stress or stroking I get there matters much to them at all. They're not impressed with any of it, good or bad; they're interested in "just plain me." In their eyes, I can be a published philosopher or whatever I choose during the day, but at the end of it all, I'm just their mom. To be with them is therefore a humbling experience — but a refreshingly restful, freeing, and humorous one. Clearing away the view of myself as an author or a speaker helps me regain my perspective and bring other, more important things into view. It's an exercise in stripping away appearances and getting back to fundamentals, where the spotlight is on the ways I can serve them rather than on the applause that serves my ego.

Magnanimity is important for Aquinas because it puts genuine greatness and true virtue in the spotlight. Loving excellence and living excellent lives bring us the task of resisting the seductions of fame and acclaim that tend to accompany excellence. If the most humble can be called to great virtue and equipped by God's grace for great things, then no one can escape vainglory by hunkering down into an unexceptional life.

If vainglory undercuts both truthfulness and magnanimity, it deserves to be called a capital vice. Living truthfully and pursuing goodness faithfully are not trivial matters. To pursue holiness within and healthy relationships with others, we must wrestle free from vainglory's twisted grip. How can we find this freedom?

CHAPTER 6

PRACTICES OF RESISTANCE, PLACES OF ENCOURAGEMENT

Until we enter quietness, the world still lays hold of us.

Dallas Willard, *Spirit of the Disciplines*

We live, in fact, in a world starved for solitude, silence, and privacy: and therefore starved for meditation and true friendship.

C. S. Lewis, *The Weight of Glory*

WHEN WE CUT the onion of vainglory and confront its multiple layers, many of us might be unable to stop ourselves from crying — or at least despairing over making real progress against this vice. How can we break vainglory's hold when our lives are broadcast from a continuous feed of fathomless pride and fear?

Evagrius, Cassian, Gregory, and Aquinas addressed an audience that was not celebrity-crazed, image-obsessed, marketing-saturated contemporary America. They designed their analyses of vainglory for a small community of Christians seriously devoted to a life of imitating Christ. These monks and friars dedicated their lives to spiritual disciplines, empowered by the Spirit, which directed their progress in sanctity. So the goods getting glory in this context were sanctity and spiritual gifts — not, as is often the case for us, youthfulness, beauty, status, or the size of our paychecks. Cassian, for example, was not too concerned with fakery and deftly manipulated audiences. Rather, he focused almost entirely on cases where glory for real virtue or genuinely honorable achievement went wrong. He knew that even people who did not seek glory could become more attached to that attention than they should. The purpose of their analyses of this vice was not self-flagellation, but freedom and flourishing. Cassian likened his work as a spiritual director to that of a doctor who not only healed those who were diseased, but also promoted practices for healthy living.[1]

Avoiding Attention

The Sayings of the Fathers records several humorous stories about monks craftily avoiding attention paid to their sanctity. Here is my favorite:

> Once a . . . judge heard of Abba Moses and went to Scete to see him. They told the old man that [the judge] was on his way, and he rose up to flee. . . . The judge and his train met him and asked: "Tell me, old man, where is the cell of Abba Moses?" And the old man said: "Why do you want to see him? He is a fool and a heretic." The judge came to the church and said to the clergy, "I heard of Abba Moses and came to see him. But an old man on his way to Egypt met me, and I asked him where was the cell of Abba Moses. And he said: 'Why are you looking for him? He is a fool and a heretic.'" And the clergy were distressed and said: "What sort of person was your old man who told you this about the holy man?" And he said: "He was an old man, tall and dark, wearing the oldest possible clothes." And the clergy said: "That was Abba Moses. And he told you this about himself because he did not want you to see him." And the judge went away much edified.[2]

It's a little ironic to read this example after our earlier comments on truthfulness and hypocrisy! But the story does show us how dangerous a risk even the most virtuous of the Fathers took vainglory to be. Can you imagine fleeing to a mosquito-infested marsh the minute you thought you might be tempted by recognition, even *deserved* recognition?

Because they understood vainglory to be a recurrent and serious problem, the early Fathers recommended several practical strategies against it — most of which did not involve sneaking off and slandering yourself before city officials. For example, you could try to avoid excessive attachment to glory by avoiding any attachments to human opinion at all. So one Desert Father offers this advice on how to make "death to the world" one's spiritual vocation:

> A brother came to see Abba Macarius the Egyptian, and said to him, "Abba, give me a word." So the old man said, "Go to the cemetery and abuse the dead." The brother went there, abused them and threw stones at them; then he returned and told the old man about it. The latter said to him, "Didn't they say anything to you?" He replied, "No." The old man said, "Go back tomorrow and praise them." So the brother went away and praised them, calling them "Apostles, saints, and righteous men." He returned to the old man and said to him, "I have complimented them." And the old man said to him, "Did they not answer you?" The brother said no. The old man said to him, "You know how you insulted them and they did not reply, and how you praised them and they did not speak; so you too if you wish to be saved must do the same and become a dead man. Like the dead, take no account of either the scorn of men or their praises."[3]

This story, like so many others in this genre of "words" or "sayings" of the Fathers, is intended to be a rhetorical slap in the face. (Some of Jesus' parables and sayings have a similar effect.) Abba Macarius helps us take seriously the importance of detachment, even radical detachment, from the scorn and praise of others. He gives us experienced counsel about how to deal wisely with both weighty and superficial words we receive from the world.

Typically when I tell this story from Abba Macarius, I feel the need to tone down his radical stance and over-the-top "dead to the world" advice. We can still take his general point, even if we aren't going to renounce the whole world, right? I recently had to rethink this apologetic approach, however. The occasion was a visit to a maximum security prison in Angola, Louisiana. My assignment: to teach a class on the vice of vainglory to a group of inmates enrolled in a seminary program there. These men, most of whom were felony offenders serving life sentences, had come to faith in Jesus Christ during their time in prison. The room was crowded: 120 men surrounded me on all sides, listening intently to the lecture, which included this "word" from Abba Macarius. At the end of the story, I was poised to finish with my usual hedge, deflating the Desert Fathers' extreme positions. But this time, as I was telling the story, a charged hush fell over the room. I delivered the punch line: "Like the dead, take no account of either the scorn of men or their praises." Then I took a breath, but before I could say another word, the whole room exploded with spontaneous applause that went on for a full minute. Preach it, Brother Macarius.

"Prison is a lonely place where you are never alone," I once heard an inmate say. In that lonely and forgotten place, where you become a Department of Corrections number, not a name, where your crime defines you and marks you with shame forever, where you are first and foremost a convicted criminal, not a human being, and where even your family eventually no longer comes to visit, these men were living out the hard-won freedom that Abba Macarius spoke of, the freedom that comes from learning to be dead to the scorn of the world. They had learned to live for the praise of God alone because that was the only place they would likely ever find a word of affirmation in this world. Before I met them, I had never realized how important it is that we serve a Savior who took on scorn and shame and mockery as well as physical pain. If you want to know Christ and the power of his resurrection, share in his sufferings. There would be no apologies for the strong words of Abba Macarius that day. To suffer humiliation was the daily discipline of these Christians. To detach from the labels the world laid on them like a heavy yoke was their spiritual work. My life is so comfortable and well-credentialed by comparison, my basic reputation and respect so automatically given that I had never thought about the pain of being without those things. Meeting these men was a convicting moment for me: I learned what detachment might really mean, and how necessary it might be for all of us, whether we're living in hard enough times to realize it yet or not.

While we need to detach, "taking no account of the scorn or praise of others," there is more to this story. After all, to live out their spiritual vocation in those fourth-century desert communities, the Fathers had to deliberately incorporate *communal* practices of reflecting on their individual spiritual progress — for example, in confession, petitionary prayers, and regular self-examination with a spiritual director. Having others pay attention to one's virtue was not only inescapable, but necessary and good, as it served to identify one's failings and to cultivate one's spiritual strengths.[4] In a parallel way, at Angola, the men who have graduated from the seminary and become pastors, serving congregations of fellow inmates with whom they not only work but live, testify that they need an authenticity of faith and an integrity of Christian walk that most of the rest of us can hardly grasp. How many of us could imagine sleeping in the same room and sharing the communal shower with those with whom we pray and worship on Sunday? The daily example of these men is a more powerful witness than their preaching, so they need faithful encouragement and regular accountability from their fellow pastors to make it through each day. Their witness, hard-won, has been fruitful: the Spirit has been working to convict others through the change they see in the men who have given their lives to Jesus in that place. As a result, the culture of Angola has been radically transformed from a violent horror to a place of hope: it is a culture of good glory.

John Cassian was tutored by the Desert Fathers, and he went on to translate their remedial practices into monastic community life. We've already seen Cassian recommend a remedy that addresses the links between vainglory and pride. He directed members of these communities to "strive utterly to reject as the stuff of boastfulness whatever is not generally accepted and practiced as part of the way of life of the brothers [in one's monastic community], and to avoid those things that could set us apart from others and that would gain us praise from human beings, as if we were the only ones who could do them."[5]

Cassian's suggestion counters the desire to gain recognition for excellences that noticeably "set us apart." Worldly reward is a danger to be avoided, not a reward to be sought. One way to prevent vainglorious temptations that arise through others' notice is to live a completely unremarkable and ordinary life or one indistinguishable from that of others — for example, following St. Benedict's *Rule* to the letter, just like every other member of one's monastery. Then one's spiritual achievements are visible only to God, "who knows what is hidden."[6] Here Cassian echoes the warnings of many Desert Fathers against attempts at heroic feats of asceticism, and Benedict follows him by teaching twelve steps of humility, by which one learns to think of oneself as lower than others.[7] Recommending a similar "rule" for all monks makes sense if we picture Simon of Stylites (a desert monk famous for his asceticism) sitting atop his pole for days on end, or Macarius returning from a week of penance in a nearby marsh so mosquito-bitten that his face is unrecognizable. Even if such practices are motivated by the desire to flee the world and its attention, such sensational practices are bound to attract the very attention they seek to avoid! Cassian's point: practices that expose us as "spiritual standouts" are — for most of us, at least — a recipe for vainglorious temptation. If we seek out such practices, we're asking for trouble. What we need to focus on instead is daily integrity in ordinary life.

Fame, Shame, and a Good Name

But even in less amazing cases than those just discussed, it can be very difficult to go unnoticed. If Aquinas is right that goodness naturally attracts attention, flying under the radar will not always be possible — nor will it be appropriate. As Augustine says, "If admiration is the usual and proper accompaniment of a good life and good actions, we ought not to renounce it any more than the good life which it accompanies."[8] We've seen that Aquinas goes even further, arguing that magnanimity's "great acts" are exercises of virtue, since God sometimes calls us to something even greater than we might have imagined for ourselves, as he did with Moses at the burning bush and Mary at the Annunciation. In these instances, you'd be showing disobedient obstinacy if you refused to serve, even if that service drew others' attention.

The Desert Fathers warn us, however, that God may intervene to chasten the vainglorious, like a parent using natural consequences to check a young child. Excessive fame-seeking is typically followed and cured by public humiliation, as noted in this passage from Evagrius:

> Whenever the [monk's] mind attains some small degree of impassibility, it then acquires the horse of vainglory and immediately rushes to the cities, getting its fill of the lavish praise accorded its repute. By providential design the spirit of fornication which came to meet him and shut him up in a pigsty teaches him not to leave his bed until he is completely healthy and not to imitate those undisciplined sick people who while still carrying about in themselves the last vestiges of sickness apply themselves to untimely walks and baths and fall back again into their illnesses.[9]

A monk, lingering over his spiritual achievements, was to check those thoughts with the mental spectacle of his public humiliation, lest vainglory send him "riding off" into the actions of shameful exposure. In other words, more publicity and a higher position of honor open us up to the potential for greater humiliation and spectacle.[10] This point is not lost on today's tabloid media, which count on celebrities in disgrace as a steady source of entertainment for their readership.[11] Riding the horse of vainglorious fame leads many to fall into the pigpen of lust and shame: Bill Clinton, Tiger Woods, Brett Favre, John Edwards, Ben Rothlisburger, General Petraeus. As the list here becomes dated, new names will no doubt be added to it.

Despite the persistence of our struggles with vainglory, with moral maturity we can learn to cope with glory, and even great fame, better over time. For his book *Fame Junkies,* Jake Halpern interviewed The Edge, the lead guitarist for the rock band U2. In the interview, The Edge noted how the band had struggled with celebrity — primarily in vainglory's fearful form — and gradually learned to handle it better:

> "After our *Joshua Tree* album, we were as famous as you could be in music," he said, "and frankly, it was kind of overpowering for a while. . . . If anything, it was something we tried to downplay. I don't think we ever really wanted celebrity in and of itself, because we came out of the whole punk rock movement, which was all about tearing that system down." More than anything else, he said, fame was a kind of psychological torment for the band, especially in the beginning. "At the big U2 concerts we were really just hanging on to make it through. There was an element of desperation in which we were just trying to focus on our music. And if we got seduced by fame, I think our version of that was being too self-conscious, taking ourselves a little too seriously, and wondering, 'Did we measure up [to the hype]? Were we a good enough band? Were we really able to do this?'"

Apparently, it took years for the band to outgrow this self-consciousness. The Edge concludes:

> "I think now that we are a little older, we just feel extremely fortunate to have such great fans and to have written some great songs. It just gets to a

93

point where you say, 'This is me. I am not everything I would like to be as an artist, but that doesn't mean I don't have anything worth saying.' Now, without being complacent, we're really enjoying what we're doing."[12]

Silence and Solitude

How do we, like U2, learn to wean ourselves off the pleasure and pressure that come with attention and adulation and keep our focus on using our gifts well? The tradition especially recommends two spiritual disciplines as pathways to virtue and practices of resistance to the vice of vainglory — the disciplines of silence and solitude.

Please note that no practice, by itself, guarantees freedom from vainglory or temptations to it. "Spiritual remedies" of the sort that Cassian and other spiritual directors suggested in their conferences were regular disciplines meant to give the Holy Spirit a fruitful occasion to work in one's heart and to help one submit to that work. They were not and are not part of a self-help regimen for supplanting God's work in us.

Still, like a soldier or an athlete (two of Cassian's favorite metaphors), we need to be aware of the threats we are facing, see where our vulnerabilities lie, and learn field-tested strategies that have proven helpful in spiritual battles and contests. Take the discipline of silence. Since we are not Trappist monks, we can expect this practice to take a wide variety of forms. Practicing silence can mean maintaining complete silence during a weekend retreat at a monastery, or setting aside one "quiet day" each week, or being silent for a shorter time (an hour before bedtime) each day. It might involve intentionally spending time in prayer, listening to and soaking up Scripture, not talking about our own needs or wants, not talking when it's not necessary for work — or even refraining from gossiping or passing along tales about others.

Not talking also implies not talking about ourselves. This cuts us off from a major mode of managing our self-presentation. It strikes us dumb — and likely also leaves us dumbfounded. We're caught up short when we confront opportunities to gain and shape others' attention and have to pass them by. Practicing silence teaches us to stop using words to project a limelight-worthy self. "Set the seal of silence on the spices of your ascetic labors," counsels Evagrius, "lest unfastened by your tongue they be stolen by esteem."[13] Practiced with regularity, silence creates space for us to be attentive to *others'* self-disclosures, including God's self-disclosure in his Word: "The silence of the Christian is listening silence, humble stillness."[14] We are likely to find it frustrating at first, but it eventually prompts us to open up healthier modes of mutual communication. Outer silence eventually silences our inner monologues and the fantasies about ourselves they prop up. When we silence our egos, we can hear God's voice more clearly in prayer, in conversation, in nature, in reading — in everything we do. As Josef Pieper notes, "Only [the one] who is silent can hear."[15]

Rather than constraining us, silence yields freedom, the freedom to stow the over-managing self on the back shelf and learn the grace of receiving. As Richard Foster puts it, "Silence frees us from the need to control others. One reason we can hardly bear to remain silent is that it makes us feel so helpless. We are accustomed to relying upon words to manage and control others. A frantic stream of words flows from us in an attempt to straighten others out. We want so desperately for them to agree with us, to see things our way. . . . We devour people with our words. Silence is one of the deepest spiritual disciplines simply because it puts the stopper on that."[16]

Here's an experiment my students and I have tried. We asked ourselves, How hard would it be to "fast" not from all words, but from speaking about ourselves? What would it be like not to talk about our feelings, frustrations, daily adventures and trials, excuses and rationalizations — not only in person, but also on Facebook, Twitter, phones, and blogs? Could we refrain from posting and tweeting and texting and blogging? Like fasting from food, this discipline requires that we give up a good thing for a time, in order to recognize the ways that our use of it or our dependence on it has become distorted and excessive. My students and I tried to practice this modified discipline of silence for one week. During that time, we were allowed to answer questions in class and have other short conversations if they did not involve comments about ourselves or express our own opinions. In cases where that was unavoidable ("How are you today?"), our protocol was to answer as briefly as possible, and then turn the conversation back toward the other person by asking about him or her.

At first, our old habits were so strong that many times we talked all about ourselves and didn't realize it until the conversation was over. Perhaps we would have done well to imitate the Desert Father who kept a pebble in his mouth as a reminder to keep his tongue tamed![17] (Some of us who had a very hard time remembering kept gum or a small piece of candy in our mouths instead.) The initial days typically brought comments from friends, usually along these lines: "Hey, are you feeling OK? You're so quiet today." As the week progressed and the quietness became normal, we became aware of two things. First, we realized how much work it was to pay attention to other people in a conversation. When you know you won't be contributing, the focus is entirely on the other, with no anticipation of providing your own feedback. Listening actively and attentively was hard for us; we were obviously out of practice. It did, however, deepen our friendships. Several students reported that they had learned all sorts of new things about those closest to them. They would never have realized or appreciated these things about others unless they had given them more time and space to speak. Second, my students realized on which occasions they rightly missed being able to share themselves through speech. At the dinner table with friends, or on the phone with their parents, who called to catch up on the week, they felt stunted by the silence. In those cases, speaking about themselves was necessary for closer relationship. And in both cases, silence revealed the ways in which communication — both speaking and allowing others to speak — was meant to draw people together. Doing this well, however, required recalibrating old habits considerably.

The students' unanimous response to this practice was that it proved extremely difficult — but was utterly convicting. In many ways it revolutionized our perspective. How much conversation did we have to give up that week? Much more than we could have imagined. How much listening did we really do when we were not being intentional about it? Much less than we thought. How many pauses or silences did we leave in conversation so that others could contribute? Far fewer than we realized. The practice of silence, even in this partial and rudimentary form, showed us that we were far *less* aware of our habits of self-aggrandizing communication than we ever imagined and much *more* in need of such regular disciplines than we could have expected.

Silence is likewise understood by spiritual writers as a space we create in our lives to hear God in prayer, as Jesus did when he retreated from the crowds to be alone with God. Adele Calhoun says, "Silence is a regenerative practice of attending and listening to God in quiet, without interruption and noise." In this practice, we "realize that the world can go on without us for an hour or a day or even longer. . . . The discipline of silence invites us to leave behind the competing demands of our outer world for time alone with Jesus. Silence offers a way of paying attention to the Spirit of God."[18] It shuts out the voices from the world we feel we need to respond to, or the voices from inside our own heads telling us about the way we need to project or protect an adequate image of ourselves. In silence and prayer, the focus is turned away from our selves and the activity of managing our human audiences. We can receive in quietness, without fear, whatever word God needs to give us.

Solitude, the second spiritual practice for resisting vainglory that I mentioned, is a similar strategy. In it, we deny ourselves not speech but an audience. Even as we withdraw from others for a time, we may find that solitude is also a positive practice for drawing near to God, just as refraining from speaking about ourselves can foster more attentive listening to others. Richard Foster describes a variety of ways of practicing the discipline of solitude: "Some draw near [to God] in the recreating silences of the early morning; others quiet themselves best in the deep quiet of the night; still others retreat from the blast of the day for a time of attentive, listening silence."[19] When my family goes on vacation to a nearby state park, I love to kayak on the lake before anyone else in the campground is awake. The water is quiet, unruffled by wind or waves, and I am warmed by the light of the rising sun. It seems easier to breathe deeply. I can soak in the world around me as a place of rest and peace. Solitude feels rich and sacred there. To retreat is to be refreshed.

Solitude may sound terrifying or boring — indeed, it may turn out to be both, initially — but it is also a powerful way to break out of the patterns and expectations of audience feedback. Without an audience, you don't have to work at getting attention from anyone. No performance is needed. No one is watching, so you can just "be yourself." If all you have become is a performer — an actor anticipating and reacting to what your audience demands — the emptiness of this self will quickly be exposed.

The project of trying to build a worthwhile self on a positive public relations platform falls flat in solitude. If you have been operating in fearful mode, solitude lifts the burden of constantly pleasing and placating. Richard Foster notes, "Solitude . . . frees us from the panicked need for acclaim and approval" and allows us to "lay down the crushing burden of the opinions of others."[20] Of course, we can attempt to substitute an imaginative fantasy audience for an actual one, as Cassian's anecdote of the monk "preaching" a magnificent sermon alone in his cell reminds us. We may even find ourselves trying to perform for God, but prolonged solitude tends eventually to expose the futility of these gestures, too.

"I am free from desiring public gaze when I need hiddenness," says Foster.[21] Why do we need hiddenness? Why does Foster need it? He confesses, "I had always prayed over decisions, and yet I too often responded on the basis of whether or not the action would put me in a favorable light. To say yes to pleas for help or opportunities to serve usually carried an aura of spirituality and sacrifice. I could say yes easily, but I did not have the ability to say no. What would people think of me if I refused?"[22] Part of what solitude does is remove us from a world in which our contributions and worth are measured by achievement, and our actions are always being assessed by others — the world as the "proving ground" of the conditionally worthy self. When we move away from others into a quiet place by ourselves, we can put their responses to us aside and simply be attuned to God's word for us.

To maintain our image before others is work (even though it often feels rewarding), but we cannot live well under the strain of this work all the time. Like Jesus, we need periods of rest and retreat from the crowds clamoring and demanding things from us, so that we can stay attentive to the Father, and thereby see ourselves more clearly, too. The Desert Fathers tell this story of three monks:

> [One of them] chose to go away and be quiet in solitude. . . . [When the first two returned,] they asked him to tell them how he himself had fared. He was silent for a while, and then poured water into a vessel and said, "Look at the water," and it was murky. After a little while he said again, "See now, how clear the water has become." As they looked into the water, they saw their own faces, as in a mirror. Then he said to them, "So is it with anyone

who lives in a crowd; because of the turbulence, he does not see his own sins: but when he has been quiet, above all in solitude, then he recognizes his own faults."[23]

Henri Nouwen describes several ways to practice solitude in his book *Making All Things New: An Invitation to the Spiritual Life.*[24] He recommends having a designated place that is quiet and distraction-free — a corner of a bedroom or a comfortable chair on a porch, or even a quiet park bench, for example. Perhaps a candle or a plant signals its being a special place, but the simpler the environment, the better. Distracting thoughts are a common problem. In her book on the spiritual disciplines, Adele Calhoun recommends imagining them as small paper boats that we simply place into a flowing river as they arise — and then let float away.[25] Nouwen also suggests having a short Scripture verse or using the Jesus Prayer as a focal point to regather our thoughts as they wander. Solitude may feel peaceful, or it may feel empty, or even like a waste of time. If we are faithful in setting aside time to be alone with God, however, we will learn to listen to God's voice, to be increasingly aware of his presence, and to notice the fruits of our solitude in the rest of our lives.

Calhoun describes solitude as both a relinquishment and a practice of replenishment and rejoicing. Relinquishment is neccessary, she says: "We need solitude if we intend to unmask the false self and its important-looking image." What happens when this image is taken away? "Without the oxygen of doing and the mirror of approval, our feelings of being real and important evaporate. Hollow places open up in our heart, and our soul feels empty and bare. . . . These disconcerting feelings can do two things for us. They reveal how much of our identity is embedded in a false sense of self. And they show us how easy it is to avoid solitude because we dislike being unproductive and unapplauded."[26]

But the relinquishment can make room for replenishment and joy. Solitude can be a practice that fills this emptiness and that teaches us to enjoy the presence of God. Calhoun compares our yearning for solitude with God as similar to the longing we had when we first fell in love — spending "time alone together" was "the way we let our beloved know that he or she mattered." So while solitude can wean us off the voices from the world we cling to in a disordered way, it can also function as a refuge from their demands: "In solitude we . . . find the truth of who we are in Christ. We are the beloved, and God is pleased with us. This identity is given; it is not earned. Many other voices pull at us, seeking to own and name us, but in solitude we learn what it is to distinguish between the voice of God and the voices of the world."[27] When Jesus returned from forty days of solitary testing in the wilderness, he came to the Jordan River to be baptized and heard God's voice clearly affirming his identity as the beloved Son.

In solitude we learn to rest in the presence of God, to enjoy the sanctuary he provides, to "quiet ourselves into the power of God."[28] As Bonhoeffer puts it, "The mask you wear before men will do you no good before him. He wants to see you as you are; he wants to be gracious to you."[29] Without a regular practice of withdrawal to re-center ourselves on what God says about us, to empty ourselves of the world's expectations and fill ourselves up with the fullness of his love, we can easily get swept up into the incessant and frantic activities of pleasing others, where the job is never done.

As with all the spiritual disciplines, there is no magic formula in which these actions will produce this or that spiritual fruit. If you find yourself exhausted by the burden of the expectations of others, or if you find yourself managing your reputation as if the world depended on it, however, the disciplines can be a way to lay down that heavy yoke. Choosing to practice silence and solitude will position us to be open to receive from God himself what we cannot engineer for ourselves, no matter how much energy we expend.

In the tradition, silence and solitude are tested practices to teach us that God's acknowledgment of us must be our center and touchstone. These practices temper our desires to display ourselves as attention-worthy and to overvalue the attention we get. When we listen to others' voices, their acknowledgment can confirm — but never replace — the divine voice. This substitutionary attempt arises out of vainglory and feeds it, but it is a futile gesture. We cannot anchor our fragile egos in the glory that human audiences give us, for it will never be enough. The Desert Fathers prescribed silence and solitude when they diagnosed a case of vainglory because these disciplines help re-align our habits of thought and desire in the direction of seeking acknowledgment and affirmation from God first and foremost. They do so by shutting off or shutting down human voices for a time (at least as much as possible). Stepping away helps us double-check whom we are relying on for affirmation, how much we want their attention, and what we want attention for.

Receiving the Gift of Glory

These disciplines certainly help strengthen our resistance to vainglory. However, the tradition clearly prescribes them for those who actually *care* about spiritual goodness and the possible corruption that attachment to glory brings. What practices would help those who, by contrast, seek attention for shallower and less worthy goods — say, fashion and fast cars? What would help reassure and re-form those who seek attention as an end in itself, rather than seeking it for genuinely approval-worthy goods? If fear as well as pride can motivate vainglory, those struggling with vain-glory of the shallower sort need something other than silence and solitude to curb their desperate attention-seeking. They need a secure sense that they are already fully known and unconditionally loved; they need to know that such knowledge and love are a gift; and most importantly, they need to trust that they have already been given that gift.

In Chapter Two I argued that people need acknowledgment and affir-mation from others as part of a well-lived human life. Vainglorious people bear witness to that need in their attempts to get glory any way they can, even in self-destructive and self-defeating ways. Those struggling with fear-based vainglory need to hear God's words of affirmation in prayer and Scripture, *and* they need to hear those words spoken through other people. If our lives are well-lived, we find ultimate affirmation only in our relationship with God. But we still learn about that affirmation by being loved by family and friends. In an article on self-respect, philosopher Robin Dillon argues that we learn to respect ourselves by experiencing others' respect.[30] Attachment studies in psychology likewise confirm that we learn that we are worthy of love through the love that those who care for us show us. Learning to love and respect ourselves is not an individual project; it is something that takes mutuality and a community of practice. I think the same idea applies in the case of acknowledgment. Rather than being directed to practice silence, then, those driven by fear to be vainglorious (and likely the rest of us, too) will need to hear the truth about their goodness spoken regularly to them, and they will need to learn to speak truthfully about themselves and their goodness in a safe community. Weaning ourselves off superficial substitutes requires acquiring a taste for the real thing. Rather than stepping away from excessive affirmation and its temptations, these fearfully vainglorious people will need to step into the right sorts of attentive communities and affirming relationships. The desert hermits agree by their own example that human community is necessary. At the end of a week of silence and solitude, monks would gather for spiritual direction, worship, and common meals. Likewise today, we need the regular nurture of authentic and personal friendships, small Bible-study groups, or accountability groups at church with whom we can be vulnerable and pray. We also need times of communal worship where our souls can be filled and refilled with the gospel message of grace and love.

A Virtuous Circle

Even with the help of spiritual disciplines like these, we should not be surprised if vainglory poses a persistent challenge, as the metaphor of the many-layered onion warns. There's no once-and-for-all cure for vice. Rather, Cassian's context — in which glory was received for *virtue* — makes handling glory rightly an ongoing task for the Christian community — even one whose members practice detachment by submitting to silence and solitude. Can we find positive practices that enable us to glory *well,* rather than, as Augustine puts it, to "find more joy in being praised than having the gift for which [we are] praised," and to be "more pleased with what [human beings] give than with what God has given"?[31]

I would love to end this chapter by confidently offering a list of failsafe positive practices that address all these forms of vainglory. But the spiritual life, lived together with other struggling human beings, is much messier than that. Instead, I offer a sermon from Augustine that he delivered later in his life, when he was serving as bishop of Hippo. He delivered it on an anniversary of his pastorate there, a special occasion that intentionally brought attention to his work shepherding his flock. It was, in other words, a classic opportunity for vainglory. So Augustine stood in the pulpit, looked at his congregation, and offered them a new confession:

> What am I to do today but present you with the danger I am in, so that you may be my joy? Now my danger is this: that I pay attention to how you praise me, and take no notice of the sort of lives you lead. But [God] knows. And it is under his gaze that I speak, under whose gaze I am not so much delighted by praise and popularity, as [I am] vexed and troubled about what sort of lives are led by those who praise me.
>
> As for being praised by those who lead bad lives, I don't want it, I shudder at it, detest it; it causes me pain, not pleasure.
>
> While as for being praised by those who lead good lives, if I say I don't want it, I will be lying; if I say I do want it, I'm afraid I may be more bent on vanity than on the solid good.
>
> So what am I to say? I don't completely want it, and I don't completely not want it. I don't completely want it, in case I should be imperiled by human praise; I don't completely not want it, in case it should mean that those to whom I preach are ungrateful. . . . So then, brothers and sisters, lighten my burden, lighten it, please, and carry it with me; lead good lives.[32]

Notice that Augustine begins his meditation focused on "the divine gaze," marking God as his primary audience. He's come a long way since those teenage years when he staked his identity on what his peers would think of him. And even though he's now in the pulpit, he's also come a long way since his years as a professionally paid rhetorician. Now he's clear that if he is to be praised, he wishes it to be for something truly good and faithfully done, something that would meet with divine approval, of which human approval would then be an apt reflection. But he has not left concerns about glory entirely in the dust of the past. Rather, Augustine thinks his goodness in faithfully carrying out his calling *should* be reflected in the good lives of those he serves and confirmed by their appropriate praise. Glory is a good thing.

What of that last line, though, in which Augustine calls on his congregation — his audience — to *lighten his burden?* It's easy to miss this point, but it's an important one. Augustine indicates that he and his congregation might best pursue a solution to vainglory together, as a *community*. His idea: handling glory well is much easier with a good audience. Aquinas defined glory as goodness that is manifest. Our goodness, when manifest, calls forth acknowledgment and affirmation from others. I'd suggest that, despite all the ways that receiving attention from others can go wrong, a mutually beneficial and edifying arrangement is possible, too. If Augustine's congregation lives good lives, of course this reflects well on God. But it also reflects well on Augustine's efforts to guide them. Further, if they are living good lives, his recognition of their goodness gives Augustine encouragement, and their recognition and praise of his good work becomes meaningful to him. In other words, their goodness makes them a good audience for him. And having a good audience helps him handle glory well. In turn, their good lives and his good shepherding together reflect well on God, bringing him glory. All those inside this community are thus mutually encouraged in their practices of virtue, and they can see the ways that their glory can build each other up. A community like this is also attractive to those outside it, and it attracts the right kind of attention for God. Vainglory may seem to trap us in a circle of vice, but that vicious circle is nothing but a distortion of an alternative *virtuous* circle — of goodness, affirmation, and praise. That is how things are meant to be.

Glorifying the Giver

Augustine's insights into remedying vainglory rely on a crucial conviction about himself and the good words he offers his congregation:

> We have our fellow poor to feed today . . . ; the rations I provide for you, though, are these words. I lack the means to feed everyone with visible, tangible bread. So I feed you on what I am fed on myself.
>
> I am just a waiter, I am not the master of the house; I set food before you from the pantry which I too live on, from the Lord's storerooms, from the banquet of that householder who "for our sakes became poor, though he was rich, in order to enrich us from his poverty" (2 Cor. 8:9).[33]

In this passage, Augustine grants that any goodness he offers to his congregation in the words of his sermon is bread from the storerooms of the Lord. So it is God's goodness which Augustine then serves to others. He cannot accept their praise properly without directing it toward the Giver of every good and perfect gift, the Giver who gave the very gift of himself, the Giver of bread and words who is himself the Bread of Life and Word of God. Through these metaphors, Augustine teaches us and his congregation that glory itself is a gift, a gift we are only stewards of, but a gift we can use to serve God and others. Our appreciation of the good things he gives us is a public witness pointing to the ultimate source of those good things.

We enjoy glory appropriately when our enjoyment of it and of all God's gifts is anchored in our identity as children of God. If we stand secure in that identity, we are free from needy grasping at a glory of our own making from whatever audience will deliver it. Augustine openly confesses his struggles with vainglory even as an old man, because he longs to be fully known by the God he loves, and he lives so securely in God's love that he knows he does not have to hide himself from others, either. Our glorying, when done well, displays our understanding of ourselves as creatures of God, always and in everything reliant on God for his gifts. Augustine is free to hand out lavish gifts and receive praise for them because he knows he is the waiter, not the master of the house; his glory-worthy actions point beyond himself. Grateful for what he has already been given, he can share his gifts of words, and when he feeds his congregation and city, it is a feast that celebrates God's goodness to them all.

Our goodness is from God and for God. Augustine's example shows that through community we can learn to value truth, goodness, and glory with rightly ordered love. Our goodness is real and really ours, a gift of love from the source of all genuine goodness, which means we need not be slaves to human opinion and the falsity and fakery characteristic of vainglory's fearful form. Our goodness is from him and for him, which means we can display, celebrate, and share our good gifts with others without the puffed-up self-promotion of vainglory's prideful form. With a focus on God's overwhelming goodness to us, we can take true delight in his gifts. Our glory story, if it is to be a good one, must be one not just of discipline set against the dangers of vice, but also of overflowing grace and gratitude. To imagine such a life lit up by grace, listen to Abba Joseph:

> Abba Lot went to see Abba Joseph and said to him: "Abba, as far as I can, I say my little office, I fast a little, I pray and meditate, I live in peace, and as far as I can, I purify my thoughts. What else can I do?"
>
> Then the old man stood up and stretched his hands towards heaven. His fingers became like ten lamps of fire, and he said to him, "If you will, you can become all flame."[34]

CHAPTER 7

SHARING THE LIGHT:
GRACE, FORMATION, AND COMMUNITY

*The "interior castle" of the human soul, as Teresa of Avila
called it, has many rooms, and they are slowly occupied by God,
allowing us time and room to grow.*

Dallas Willard, *The Divine Conspiracy*

*I think it is hope that lies at our hearts and hope that finally
brings us all here. . . . . Hope that we are known, each one of us by
name, and that out of the burning moments of our lives he will
call us by our names to the lives he would have us live and the
selves he would have us become. . . .*

Frederick Buechner, *Secrets in the Dark*

GLORY CAN BE good, a gift to God and to each other. When vice
distorts our desires for it and nourishes them with pride and fear, we
build resistance to those distorted desires with disciplines like silence and
solitude. But in this battle of heart and mind, are you a gladiator alone
in the arena, or a comrade in arms with a full battalion beside and behind
you? Even more, is this *your* fight or the Lord's?

I'll be the first to admit that it's hard, especially for Protestants, to
think about the program of vices and spiritual disciplines without also
worrying that grace gets short shrift. Isn't the work of setting us free from
sin already completed by Jesus Christ on the cross? Isn't the transformation of our hearts really the work of the Holy Spirit? So why belabor all
these fine distinctions among types and sources of vainglory to discern

our sin and confess it in tedious detail? Why spend pages explaining how to practice resistance to the vainglorious habits entrenched in our lives? These approaches focus too much on human efforts, on what *we* see and what *we* should do — so this objection goes. And if that's true for vainglory, is it true for the whole tradition of thinking and talking about the vices?

Good questions. When it comes to sin and sanctification, we need to get things straight, most importantly because they determine the answer to the most important question of all: *How do we live* as redeemed disciples of Jesus Christ? In the rest of this chapter, I'll address the objection that identifying and resisting our vices overshadow the power of grace. Then I'll raise two more concerns, both of which redirect our attention from the mark that vainglory inks on the character of individual Christians (my focus in the book so far) to its communal and cultural fingerprints. Augustine's sermon in the previous chapter already hinted at vainglory's *social* character, an idea that should spur communities to craft structural remedies and shape cultural climates that foster good desires, to complement the efforts of individuals practicing spiritual disciplines. Along with that challenge, we also need to see if vainglory-vice talk applies on the *secular* stage, among those who aim to "leave a legacy" or "make a splash" without giving God even a minor role. Can those who do not share any limelight with God recognize what makes vainglory a vice?

Sin, Sanctification, and Spiritual Disciplines

A Labyrinth of Sin?

The Desert Fathers stood in a particular Christian community at a particular moment in history, pouring their energy into naming and learning to diagnose the vices, teasing apart their roots and offspring vices, and prescribing antidotes. Given the distance of centuries and the developments of the faith, it might be a stretch to transplant their approach into our lives — and it's not obvious that it would be beneficial. Are Cassian's and Gregory's "sin-diagnostic systems" the best way to think about the Christian life for us, today? From Evagrius to Aquinas up to the Reformation, the tradition gives us catalogs of sins — capital or principal vices and their offspring (often in neat sets of sevens), mortal and venial sins, penitential manuals and trees of vices. It can be a dizzying array of lists, leading into a labyrinth of diagnostic tests and aids to confession. Studying them can leave us breathless, overwhelmed, and paralyzed by the sheer magnitude and detail of all the things that can be wrong with us. How helpful is that, really? Moreover, isn't our own sin something we can never fully grasp, given the depths of our ignorance, blindness, and self-deception (which are themselves likely also effects of sin)? Remember the Psalmist, who asks, "Who can discern his errors? Forgive my hidden faults" (Ps. 19:12). Indeed, we should not assume that careful diagnosis of and extensive rumination on the type of sin we struggle with will actually help us overcome it. That is the Lord's work. Rather than analyzing each sin and paging through penitential manuals at laborious length to get to the bottom of each individual offense, wouldn't it be healthier and more theologically sound to simply confess our sinful condition generally, trust Christ's sacrifice to wash it all away, and entrust ourselves thereafter to God's forgiveness and the Spirit's healing?

These are the questions of pastors, counselors, and others who have seen people struggle with sin and get caught in webs of self-accusation, shame, and guilt from which they feel unable to escape. They know, as we do, that dangerous excesses are possible and, in plenty of cases, actual. For example, the thirteenth-century Dominican William Peraldus wrote a treatise on the seven deadly sins that included twenty-seven chapters on sloth and its symptoms alone. Can you imagine facing confession with a priest armed with such a list of possible wrongdoing? Even thinkers within the Catholic tradition point out the skewed focus of the manualists: too much emphasis on sin and too little on grace and practices of regeneration.[1] No wonder Martin Luther spent hours in the confessional, sorely trying the patience of his confessor as he attempted to identify and recount the faults of just one day! There is, however, a better way.

Apprentices in Christlikeness

One of the reasons I take the work of Thomas Aquinas on the vices as a touchstone is that he articulates as clearly as anyone the *positive* project into which analysis of the vices fits. He organizes the ethical part of his masterwork, the *Summa theologiae,* around the seven virtues. These traits perfect us into the likeness of Christ; the virtues form the backbone of Christian living. To become virtuous, Aquinas says, is simply to grow into more Christ-like character, for Jesus is the model of virtue, the one with perfected human nature. Through Christ and for his sake, God gives us his Spirit to aid us in living virtuously.[2] That means the work of Christ and the work of the Holy Spirit are foundational to our efforts to live into closer and closer communion with God. On Aquinas's picture of the moral life, therefore, we are not obsessing over "the sin that so often entangles" (Heb. 12:1). He, like many others in the Christian tradition, steadfastly keeps his focus on the imitation of Christ (Eph. 5:1), the perfect example of virtue who shows us "in his own person" how to live abundantly in full communion with God.[3]

For Evagrius, Cassian, Augustine, and Aquinas, the pursuit of virtue is a Spirit-empowered, Spirit-enabled adventure. Evagrius says,

> As for those who have received from grace the strength for ascetic labors, let them not think that they possess this from their own power, for the word of the commandments is for us the cause of all good things, just as the Deceiver is for evil suggestions. For the good things you accomplish, therefore, offer thanksgiving to the cause of good things. . . . At the conclusion of every work, dedicate your thanksgiving to [God]. . . . For he who has joined thanksgiving to action will possess inviolable the treasure of his heart.[4]

Cassian recommends this regimen: "In the case of each virtue where we have felt that we have made progress, we speak the words of the Apostle: 'Not I, but the grace of God with me.' And: 'By the grace of God I am what I am.' And that it is God 'who works in us both to will and to accomplish, for the sake of his good pleasure.'" To use his athlete-of-Christ metaphor: "For the willing and running of no one, however fervent and desirous he might be, could be sufficient for one who is girded with a flesh that resists the spirit, such that he would be able to obtain the great prize of perfection and the palm of integrity and purity, unless he were protected by the divine mercy so as to deserve to attain that which he greatly desires and to which he runs."[5] Human efforts to "take off the vices" and "put on the virtues" (Col. 3; Eph. 4) depend on the Spirit's work and cannot in any way supplant it.

But this does not mean that no effort is required on our part. Living as apprentices in Christlikeness does not mean lying on the couch waiting for the Holy Spirit to wave a magic wand to make us holy. As Scripture puts the point, grace and effort go together: "*His divine power has given us everything we need for life and godliness. . . . For this very reason, make every effort* to add to your faith goodness . . ." (2 Pet. 1:3, 5; my emphasis). Just as we regularly engage in worship, confess, study the Scriptures, offer our gifts, and pray, so all of our "practices" can lead us toward Christ-like virtues and away from the vices. This is not working for our own salvation; it is working out the faith we have already been given by walking in step with the Spirit.

Sin Systems and Pastoral Practices

Even if we are mindful of spiritual formation as the goal and of grace as the essential means, there are still ways to turn sin and self-examination into an overwhelming system. To counter this concern, I suggest that we learn how the list of vices was originally used. That will give us a clue about how to best use this catalog today.

By the time Aquinas entered the conversation about the vices in the thirteenth century, the tradition had built the vices into a complicated system over almost a millennium. It had a simple beginning. Evagrius drew his fourth-century list of vices from Christ's wilderness temptations. Occasionally he singled out a "top three" in an otherwise flexible and fluctuating list of eight or sometimes nine vices. As time went by, thinkers built on and further theorized the practical wisdom of the desert. Cassian, Evagrius's disciple, ordered his list of eight vices from those with the most carnal objects (gluttony, lust) to those with the most spiritual objects (vainglory, pride). A few centuries later, Gregory the Great reworked Cassian's list of eight to make pride the root of the remaining seven capital vices. He also added seven offspring to each of the seven capital vices — so everything would fit the theological tradition's standard "system of sevens" (seven virtues, seven petitions of the Lord's Prayer, seven Beatitudes, seven spiritual and corporal works of mercy, and so on).

And that is before the manualists spun those catalogs into lengthy lists of questions for the confessional (an example: "Envy: of neighbor? of brother? of those in authority?; regarding physical qualities? regarding spiritual qualities?; expressed in thought? word? deed?"). Given the vices' long history of accretions, we might rightly wonder whether all the lists and catalogs are, by our day, so ridiculously detailed that they have eclipsed any space in the conversation for goodness or grace.

The messiness and manifold accretions may be partly due to the way the list fluctuated — which was the result of the list's origin in Christian desert practices of spiritual direction, not a scriptural source text. For Protestants, for whom Scripture is a *sine qua non,* that missing piece may make that system suspect. Many of the vices are mentioned (or exemplified) outright in the Old and New Testaments, but others, like sloth, are much harder to find. Still others, like greed, get lots of attention in Scripture, but less consistent scrutiny in the tradition. Nor does the traditional list of seven vices match any of Paul's New Testament "sin lists." (See, for example, Rom. 1:28-32; Gal. 5:19-21; Eph. 4:31; Col. 3:5-9.) As a result, Protestants tend to build their analyses of sin around the Ten Commandments. For a counterbalancing list of virtues, they would substitute the fruits of the Spirit (Gal. 6), even though the pedigree of the list of seven virtues is at least partly biblical.[6]

What to say in response to these suspicions and this over-systematizing of sin? I'd suggest we return to the beginning. The list of capital vices originated in an intentionally Christian community and was intended to be used for the monks' program of forming disciples as "athletes" and "soldiers" of Christ, able to live in unhindered communion with God. In this program, a spiritual director's scrutiny of one's soul using the vice rubric was meant for help and healing. Rather than plunging monks into an obsession with sin from which they could never emerge, the vice lists were essential tools for discernment, both by spiritual directors and by those they counseled. To know the vices within was to beware of the weapons and wiles of the devil.

Just as Christ went through temptation in the wilderness as a stage of preparation for his ministry, so the monks patterned their lives after his example. Diagnosing and resisting their vices was the first, preparatory stage. In the "practical life," the monks engaged in disciplines meant to target areas of spiritual weakness and to teach restraint of distracting passions so they could pursue holiness with greater singleness of purpose — what Cassian called "purity of heart." This first stage and its practices prepared monks for stage two, "pure prayer" or contemplation of God. Like toddlers who are taught by parents to control their impulses and outbursts, to share, to use good manners, and so on, the monks developed spiritually toward greater maturity, helped along by prescribed practices and patient instruction from their spiritual "fathers." This process was preparation for "adulthood," a life of mature faith and a deeper union with God. Of course, the monks were realistic enough to admit that no one could completely conquer or purge temptations to vice from his or her life; setbacks were part of everyone's experience. "Purity" was a goal, one not fully attained this side of the grave. Nevertheless, to live as a disciple was to expect overall spiritual progress.

There's a pattern here. Both the Desert Fathers and Aquinas located discernment of one's vices in a much larger, positively oriented virtue program — one aimed at fostering closer and closer communion with God. Discipline is part of relationship that is growing in maturity. If we are concerned about becoming burdened by or preoccupied with our sin, we need to remember the bigger picture. Confessions and spiritual disciplines are helpful tools, the means to spiritual growth. Confronting sin is not an end in itself. Think of a coach analyzing film from last week's football game. He identifies his players' weaknesses and mistakes. Then he puts them through drills meant to strengthen them where they need it most, all so they'll play a better game, and even win, the next week. This process is a coordinated, communal effort. Often the training takes time, and everyone puts in much practice before they can see the results in a better performance. The important thing to remember is that the diagnosis and the drills of the spiritual life are part of a developmental program of dying and rising, developing and re-forming disciples who are capable of loving God more and more faithfully.

The vices list wasn't designed to be a Scripture commentary, invented by theoreticians and theologians in a university system. It wasn't an intellectual exercise. The list arose from desert *practice.* Imagine someone today who ministers to people in a Christian counseling center for thirty years, and, at the end of her career, determines the top five issues she observed people struggling with. Then imagine her writing these down, along with her experiences of which therapies were most effective in helping people deal with these struggles, and which patients were helped and why. That's a pretty good picture of how the lists of sins started. Evagrius was an apprentice who inherited a wealth of desert experience from his masters in Egypt. He compiled it and wrote it down, adding his own counsel to their collective wisdom. Despite Cassian's work at ordering the list into a progression from carnal to spiritual vices, he freely admitted that people wrestle with different vices in varying orders. In fact, making too much of sin as a "system" undercuts the list's primary purpose: to serve as a helpful rubric that pastorally sensitive spiritual care-givers can use to help real struggling individuals.

Soul Care

Cassian's own picture of his work is like that of a doctor. Medical school is necessary and helpful, but it is no substitute for clinical practice, where a doctor must treat particular patients who present both familiar and puzzling symptoms. The vices list is meant to aid our diagnoses of these "spiritual maladies" or diseases, which are then brought before Christ, the "Physician of souls," for healing. It turns out, says Cassian, that the very methods used for healing certain maladies also make good preventative care, not only blocking the recurrence of disease but also building healthy habits for future well-being. To continue the physician's metaphor: It's much like a diet and exercise regimen designed to lower cholesterol.

So the lists were meant as a heuristic aid in Christian counseling or spiritual direction — what the tradition called "soul care" (analogous to our "health care"). They did not intend to provide an exhaustive or ranked or systematic list of all possible sins, or even the worst possible sins. Rather, they helped articulate problems for those who knew vaguely that there was something wrong, but couldn't name it or pinpoint the source of their struggle, like a patient who goes to the doctor with symptoms of persistent abdominal pain, wondering whether it is simple indigestion or something more serious. The doctor helps the patient to name the trouble and take steps to cure it. Similarly, when we name our sins, we take a powerful step forward in "taking off the sinful self, with its practices" and "putting on the new self, created to be like Christ." As N. T. Wright points out, this is intentional work — work that requires knowledge, insight, and discernment (Phil. 1:9-11).[7]

Wright also follows the Fathers in recognizing that discernment and discipleship are the work of a Christian community, not of an individual. We often cannot see our own sins, and even when we have a sense that things are wrong, we don't always have a name for the problem. At other times, we do have a name for specific sins of ours and need to confess them — not only in communal and more general confession in worship, but also in more personal confession to others, to receive their words of counsel and grace as God's word to us. I have a Christian friend who meets with me once a week. We share our lives, our struggles, our worries, our joys. We pray with and for each other. The two of us function, in our small and imperfect way, as the sort of community that the Desert Fathers intentionally lived in. When I confess my sin to her, she offers me a sometimes surprising, often illuminating view of my faults. Her experience from a place on the road just ahead of me gives her wisdom to share, and with her I experience the power of prayer with a fellow traveler. We read and pray Scripture together, and we avail ourselves of other Christian resources to make sense of our lives. We are being formed as disciples together. The tradition's writings on vainglory offer us just such a resource. In the context of such a loving relationship, we are not studying a system to slavishly crank through, but discovering how to grow closer to Jesus Christ and how to be like him. Once we understand the history of the vices, we can sort original intent from subsequent abuses. We will see that what the best of our well-traveled mentors offer is not a paralyzing labyrinth of sin, but a treasury of guidance and wisdom for the journey ahead.

It is equally important to remember that this journey is one of sanctification, not of finding salvation. Resisting vices and cultivating virtues, in a Christian context, is the work of a disciplined disciple — someone who is already accepted by the Master and who is now for that reason enrolled in the school of training-in-righteousness. We do not take off the vices by our own effort in order to make ourselves pure enough for God to give us saving faith. "Saving faith," another term for "justification," is a gift of grace offered to us by the redeeming work of Jesus Christ in his death and resurrection. When we receive the gift of faith, however, it is not as though we have nothing more to do until we die. God's gifts of faith and grace and divine power are *for* something — for transforming us into a new creation. The vice and virtue lists offer helpful ways of breaking down that process of transformation into portions we can wrap our minds around. It's like a musical conductor correcting his instrumentalists' intonation, recommending specific drills, like scales played with a metronome, noting tricky sections of the score, and coordinating rhythms in disparate parts of an orchestra so they can play a symphony together in beautiful harmony. The point of breaking the music and parts down is to put them back together again into a better-integrated whole.

Vainglory's Social Side

Communal enterprises like athletic teams and musical ensembles are the right metaphors, for disciples are not isolated individuals, but part of the Body of Christ. Thinking of the Christian life as a social enterprise shifts our focus from vainglory as a purely individual or personal problem — our primary focus so far — to the way vices are communally fostered and communally resisted. Vainglory, while certainly a personal, individual spiritual problem, also warps structures and does institutional damage in society and culture.[8]

Don't we feel the sting of disappointment when the business we work for rewards only high-profile contributions by those who fit the traditional leadership mold, while our invisible labor goes unmentioned and unappreciated? Who our company celebrates and what sorts of achievements it acknowledges implicitly encourage us to be concerned with a certain kind of reputation and certain practices of self-promotion (or self-presentation). A "get-ahead" genre of books promises to teach us how. Even when we consciously shun the reward systems we live in, we still long for real recognition. Does our essential behind-the-scenes work really matter to anyone?

We face a different problem when our employers expect and even require employees to uphold a certain company image. Sometimes the disconnect between who we are and the face we have to wear in public makes us squirm. Our kids are learning to craft their self-images according to anticipated social rewards on the playground and online. How do social media encourage expectations of instant audience response and routinize all sorts of information about ourselves? When we digitally capture and post every event our children participate in from their babyhood on, do we unwittingly send a message that everything they do is a performance for an adoring audience? With cameras in every electronic device we pocket, how can they avoid living as if they were actors and performers? What if we want a day off or some privacy? The difficulty — given both the internal craving and the external social pressure — of opting out for a time brings home the startling fact of how ubiquitous these social demands and our visceral responses to them really are.

When we watch TV sitcoms, we learn the witty put-down and hear incessant cues to laugh or cheer. Commercials pair images with reputations: people at bars and beaches in beer ads are fun and laughing and beautiful, neat-and-organized mothers have spic-and-span kitchens and perfectly pressed clothing, rough-and-tough males drive rugged pickup trucks, business executives get reports and dictate orders while walking briskly to their next meeting, working women look harried but attractive in heels and tight-fitting suits. Whether we like it or not, they also teach us, by contrast, that when we fail to mimic these images, our painfully awkward self-display will earn us shame and cut us off from others' esteem and approval (like *Seinfeld*'s George, who will never, ever get a decent date). These images shape our self-image and the image we want to project to others. Led by the example of rock stars and movie stars, teens use Twitter and Instagram to cultivate their own following, and screaming, face-painted sports fans revel in ritualized chants and spectacles designed to signal their identity as loyal fans. Because these are social rituals and institutionalized practices, the draw of vainglory here is not a simple matter of individual weakness. Our culture forms us to crave recognition. Our social world — online and in person — is a whirl of attention-seeking, an expected way of life. Vainglory is a social vice; its pollution is the very air we breathe.

The more opportunities for publicity we have, the more problems with vainglory we potentially face. This makes our contemporary culture a breeding ground for vainglory. Are twenty-first-century Americans therefore more vulnerable to socialized vainglory than, say, medieval friars or desert monks? It might seem obvious that we are. How could a life spent in desert solitude or the medieval cloister possibly be more difficult than constant exposure to media designed to make every corner of our personal lives and preferences a moment ripe for publicity? True, vainglory's shallow and superficial forms tempt us more easily and often now. And it's true that culturally we are encouraged to vainglorious show, for example, in what we purchase and what we wear. Additionally, the media's ubiquitous sensationalizing of everything can certainly dull our sense of what is truly worthy of glory.

This same culture, however, perhaps because it trades so well in the shallow and sensational, is starved for virtuous substance. Trading daily in our culture's impoverishment limits our spiritual discernment by desensitizing us to the more spectacular forms of vainglory. Those preoccupations may also limit our wise reflection on what is excellent, and noble, and beautiful. In so doing, they may also block more subtle serious forms of vainglory from our view. How can we promote our own virtue if we don't have much? And it might not even occur to us that virtue is promotion-worthy material, since these days it's branded as stuffy and boring. Who prefers to read about fifty years of faithfulness in marriage when there is a tooth-and-claw celebrity divorce in the headlines? Since there is less opportunity for public display in a solitary desert cell, and the image one hopes to project is so different, the desert monks' preoccupations with vainglory certainly took a strikingly different form. Our predicament and preoccupations are perhaps thus the opposite of theirs. We live and breathe vainglory's flashy forms, with a constant virtual audience for whatever we say and do toted wherever we go via smartphone, while the monks dealt in silence with vainglorious fantasies of virtue in their own heads. Since we cannot or will not flee to the desert, what is the best response to the culture of socially embedded vainglory?

Practices of Encouragement and the Poison of Envy

While the spiritual disciplines of solitude and silence considered in Chapter Six are indeed helpful in exposing vainglory and resetting spiritually healthy patterns in our hearts and minds, the tradition often addresses them to individual Christians in intentional settings of individual self-examination. But communities and social structures can help individuals resist vainglory, too, especially when it is an undercurrent running through social practices we take for granted.

As a student of mine once insightfully noted, solitude and silence are disciplines in which we *withdraw* from broken forms of community, disciplines that detach us from sin-warped social systems of recognition and reward. What disciplines, in contrast, would *bring us back* into healthy community? What would heal those social structures and build communities that can offer Christian encouragement, rightly ordered toward God's glory? What positive practices could not only push against vainglory but also pull us toward virtue?

In the rhythm of the church calendar, the major periods of fasting — Advent and Lent — are followed by the two greatest feast days of the church, Christmas and Easter. Can we imagine a "fast" of silent solitude from disordered, manipulative, false, self-aggrandizing communication followed by a "feast" of appropriately up-building, true, God-glorifying celebration and grateful encouragement within the Christian community? If we take our cue from the sermon of Augustine presented in Chapter Six, what would it look like to become a "good audience" for those who might otherwise be susceptible to vainglory? For one thing, it might involve practices of listening and attending to others. Josef Pieper recommends becoming more attentive and able to take in what is around you.[9] This usually requires stilling concerns about how others perceive you and turning your focus toward receiving their gifts and goodness.

When we practice "taking in" goodness from others, we will find things to celebrate together. Think of a time in your life when there was a true celebration. A group sharing their sheer joy openly. Sharing appreciation for a gift, or for goodness — perhaps even a goodness not worth celebrating in the world's eyes. Was it a baptism or a first communion? A funeral eulogy? A birthday surprise out of the blue from a friend to let you know how much your friendship meant to her? Or think of lower-key celebrations of a more everyday sort: an office that cheers its members' successes at the beginning of its monthly meetings, a handshake and a word of respect after a completed project at work, a morale-boosting high-five of encouragement between team members after a setback in a game, a reassuring hug and a shared moment of relief when a high-pressure public performance (and the hours of preparation that let up to it) are finally over.

Let's be honest: it's not always easy for us to celebrate goodness together. Often we struggle to "rejoice with those who rejoice" because their successes seem to dim our own. When glorying together goes bad, what goes wrong? What prompts us to resent another who receives attention? Gregory the Great explains how vainglory is closely connected to the vice of envy, which is the habit of resenting others' goodness because it exceeds our own and therefore makes us feel inferior: "Because . . . [the vainglorious one] is seeking the power of an empty name, [he] feels envy against anyone else being able to obtain it."[10] We cannot help but notice that a rival's goodness exceeds our own when that goodness gets special notice, when the comparison is shown and made known to all. It's our inferiority on public display as much as another's superior excellence — just the sort of excellence that naturally attracts attention. And we hate to suffer by comparison. Celebrating his or her achievement feels like putting a knife in our own back.

Our culture is especially competitive. Because so many of those competitions are public, it is perilously easy to feel like we can't be good unless we're better than another, as judged and confirmed by an audience. We even make love relationships competitive — witness *The Bachelor* and *The Bachelorette* series broadcast on TV. The shows *Survivor* and *The Apprentice* are metaphors for our lives: social acceptance is performance-based, competitive, and fickly dependent on others' whims and prejudices. Starved for unconditional love, we find ourselves waiting to be voted off the island and checking the "like" versus "dislike" counts on our YouTube and Facebook posts for an ego boost several times a day. Films and love songs express our yearning for promises of a lifetime of love, but the reality we live in is littered with shards of shattered commitments. Biblically speaking, we are like Leah, wondering but never knowing how it would feel to be loved like Rachel; we are like Joseph's brothers, yearning for our father's special love but believing we will never have it.

Does this cultural formation infect the church community? We all know it does. Why do we feel shame in sharing the story of our prodigal child, our marital struggles, or the pornography habit we just can't kick? It doesn't help that we are surrounded by others with perfectly behaved, church-attending children, that our Christian bookstores tout volumes about happy couples enjoying strong, loving relationships, and that we are met with condemnation, not compassion, when we reveal our dirty little secrets and confess that the power of prayer hasn't revolutionized our lives yet. Is there an unconscious competition going on? Why do we feel the need to keep up with the just-a-little-more-Jesus-y Joneses? Most of us would much rather appear to be successful disciples than have to plead our cause with "Jesus, friend of sinners." Our own sin makes us ashamed. It's not something we like to reveal — even in worship. When others shine for Jesus, sometimes it just shows our own darkness in greater relief.

Aquinas writes that envy's offspring vices are a tendency to rejoice when others fail and a tendency to sulk when others succeed. If we cannot shake our envy, public acclaim of the goodness of others will be an occasion of sin, not of celebration. Vainglory's publicity-mongering exacerbates the envy that lingers in our hearts. It is salt in our wounds.

Envy is cured only when our sense of worth is grounded in the unconditional love of God. With that secure foundation, we can receive and celebrate gifts in ourselves and others without envy, because no gift (and no amount of attention for it) makes us more or less accepted or loved by God. Our inferiority and superiority in this or that area is not the barometer of our dignity or worth. Taking this deeply rooted love to heart gives us freedom to embrace and celebrate God's gifts as gifts to all of us — as common goods, not competitive goods. Is it any accident that vainglory and envy have a similar cure? When our self-love is grounded on the secure foundation of God's love for us, we are free from excessive neediness for others' attention and from the desire to "out-compete" others for more affirmation.

When it is our good that a community celebrates, are we primed to offer it to others as a gift and a common good? Both giver and receiver need to think of goodness as something that can be shared. This is countercultural and something we need to practice, especially in the church. Let me offer one example. After I gave a talk on vainglory, one audience member asked me a practical question: How can you take a compliment well? Do you downplay your achievement? Do you squirm (or glow) when you're praised? She suggested an alternative: Simply express your delight that the other person appreciated what is good and offer in return your appreciation of the way the compliment encouraged you. So she might say, "I found your work on this so interesting and helpful." And I could respond, "Thank you for sharing your kind words with me. It was a pleasure to do this work. Hearing that it's helped you gives me great encouragement." In this way, we show how each person's gift is a gift to all, and glory is genuinely exchanged as a blessing to both members of the body.

Lost in Translation: Vainglory as a Secular Vice

Thinking about vainglory as a social vice with a social cure leads us to one last issue: in what societies is a cure possible — sacred or secular or both? Obviously the Desert Fathers who named vainglory and gave it a prominent place on the list of vices were Christians trying to turn away from desires that derailed their full devotion to God. Thinkers like Aquinas who carried the concept forward likewise examined vainglory within the framework of Christian discipleship and spiritual formation. This history raises a question: Is vainglory so tied to its original context that it is untranslatable outside the Christian tradition?

Compare the treatment other vices get in non-Christian conversations today. Many people consider lust and gluttony matters of individual prerogative, not tendencies that wreak serious spiritual damage. Sometimes they're even seen as perfectly natural physical desires, so that those who prohibit them are scoffed at for being body-haters, misguidedly presuming to inhibit pleasures that human beings are meant to experience. If people don't acknowledge that our bodies are parts of the One Body and that our lives should honor Christ, what appeals would convince them, beyond concerns about health and social propriety? Or, on the other hand, is vainglory more like the vice of wrath or the vice of envy, which tend to count as perennial problems even for non-Christians (and the non-religious), even if they are now addressed with therapy instead of confession? In general, people concede that wrath is a destructive habit leading to violence and abuse, and you don't have to be a psychologist to admit envy's corrosive effects on personal relationships. Could vainglory enjoy the same sort of crossover acknowledgment as a vice?

Part of what makes this question acute is the theological claim that glory does not belong to us alone. As we've already seen in this book, it's a hallmark of Christian teaching that all goodness comes from God; the goodness we have is a gift, and is good only insofar as it participates in and reflects God's goodness. For those reasons, all glory — if it is to be well-ordered and rightly appreciated — must ultimately be directed to God. In this view, human glory is always a derivative good, one that reflects God's glory. If you denied this basic claim, would we have any other grounds on which to convince you that it would be morally disordered to glory in your own goodness?

Glorying in "vain things" — like glorying in goods we don't have (fake goods) and glorying in superficial or shallow things (fluff) — might still count as morally problematic, especially in cases where we seriously stake our egos on such attention. Outside Christian contexts, we still routinely use "vanity" and "being vain" as terms of moral disapproval when someone's puffed-up self-image outstrips his or her real worth. We still teach our children to condemn the queen in *Snow White.* (Notice, though, that women's magazines simultaneously encourage mothers to obsess over beauty and plant themselves in front of mirrors — there's the social-formation side of vainglory again.) Americans also tend to scorn any tint of hypocrisy in favor of "being true to oneself" — what Charles Taylor calls the "ideal of authenticity"[11] — and we prize our individual freedom to rise above conformity to others' opinions, to uphold the ideal of autonomy. Further, in the brightest moments of media limelight, we respect and applaud (and even expect) people who win awards to express gratitude to friends and supporters in their acceptance speeches. Those who do not make grateful speeches are viewed as self-centered, in a way that counts as something more than a breach of etiquette. For some sports fans, NBA basketball star LeBron James may never live down the publicity feat of airing his choice to play for the Miami Heat in an exclusive show starring himself that ESPN called "The Decision," even if his return to play in Cleveland later was less sensationalized. And here's one more example: contemporary psychology labels extreme forms of narcissism — which shares some notable symptoms with vainglory — as diagnosable disorders. These examples show us that Americans who endorse authenticity, autonomy, and gratitude have a cultural value system that enables them to recognize that vainglory is a threat to those values.

The End of Good Glory

But remember Augustine's critique of the Romans. In a Christian view, if we claim that our goods and glory are "all about us," we have fallen into a sort of idolatrous pride. This is a diagnosis that by definition requires reference to our relationship with God. Any attention we revel in as belonging to us (without qualification) on account of our own goodness (without qualification) is a good that we desire in a disordered way, because we fail to see its (and our) essential dependence on the source of goodness. God is an essential piece of the puzzle explaining how we glory "in vain." Even in a secular system of value which recognizes some "vain" sorts of glorying, glory's ultimate end does not square up.

So where does that leave a secular definition of vainglory? Back in the equivalent of an honor culture like that of the Romans, in which "having our name go down in history" could be unapologetically affirmed as a good end and could take its place among other worthwhile human goals? Think again of the bride-to-be who walks away with her ring and forgets her beloved; the same sort of problem arises. The things we get glory for are goods, and glory for them can be a good, but things still get fundamentally twisted when their goodness becomes disconnected from the source of goodness. When we disregard their signaling or reflecting function, we have lost sight of what they — and we — are *for.*

We can't understand vainglory fully without understanding the way this vice misdirects glory to the wrong end: ourselves. And without that form of vainglory in view, we can't understand its character as a *capital* vice — the pursuit of a good that we build our life around instead of God.[12] Augustine argued that this is essentially a spiritual problem. When we are vainglorious in this way, we claim exclusively and independently for ourselves what is God's right and due. This picture of glory can't be fixed with a trivial tweak: what this picture misses is nothing less than the root of all the capital vices: pride. Our goodness is genuinely good, but it is not, ultimately, only ours. That is the point of using gift language. If the goodness is a gift from God, and glory rightly attaches to that good gift when it reflects back on the Giver, then making glory self-referential rather than relational misses the main point. (Christianity also assumes that the kinds of goodness and glory we are rightly concerned with are common goods, not competitive goods, which should make their celebrations distinctive.)[13] If Augustine is right, and I think he is, we have to define vainglory in theological terms. Perhaps this is partly what explains our culture's lack of vocabulary for this vice today.[14]

Then what's left? Let's imagine that in our cultural context we could maintain a category of vainglory that covers "vain things" (faked goods, for example). Even if a secularized concept of vainglory would do the job in these cases, note that it could not work in cases of glory gained for *virtue* — that is, cases in which we receive glory for a genuine spiritual good. If we gloried in our virtue without any reference to grace, we'd be like the Romans or the Pharisees, for whom virtue was valued for the sake of personal acclaim. That would be to corrupt the virtue we are supposed to be celebrating. Of course, that we value virtue, not its cheap imitation, is still worth something. If, however, glory is our *ultimate* aim, it's not clear why virtue itself would be more valuable than its mere appearance: this aim seems to make the slide toward vainglory more tempting, not less. Perhaps the progression from virtue to vainglory that Augustine and Aquinas portray is a pattern we should expect when we disconnect goodness from its source. In short, while certain kinds of vainglory will sometimes be recognizable as vice from a secular point of view, they're mostly the trivial ones — not the ones with the most moral and spiritual significance.

Glorious Occasions for Grace

At this point, we seem to have reached an impasse. I'd like to say something more hopeful here. If virtue is developmental, this may give us a possible way forward. Our culture admits that we should express gratitude when the good things we have and do depend on others, so it has some resources to move us beyond a purely selfish kind of glorying to a more communal notion of how we should appreciate and give glory for goodness. Against the myth of the "self-made man," we can become more conscious of the ways that human goodness "points beyond itself," if only to indicate its dependence on the contributions of many.

The photo of the beautiful sunset depends on the photographer's eye but also on the technology she uses. The virtuosic performance of Brahms' first piano concerto depends not only on the pianist and his practice, but also on years of instruction by skilled teachers who gave lessons paid for by parents, institutions supported by countless patrons of the arts, the creators and craftspeople who made the instrument, and — let's not forget — the talent of the composer himself! Even the chance to perform is contingent on others' love of music and willingness to pay for tickets. The more you think about it, the fewer cases of purely *individual* glory there are. Attending to this wider web of goodness moves us toward greater moral maturity. It is also a healthy step away from the most obvious forms of vainglory. And most people would agree that children can and should be formed morally in this direction, with the aid of good teaching, social reinforcement, practice in good manners, and so on.

The next move would be to enlarge our sense of dependence on others from our immediate community — mentors, supporters, teachers, and so forth — to an even more expansive community, one that eventually includes a source of goodness beyond human action altogether. Take the feeling we get when we are part of something much, much bigger than ourselves. Think of the Olympic athlete, for example, who weeps when she hears the national anthem crown her victory, overwhelmed by gratitude, knowing her time at the Games is made possible by the support of an entire town back home, and seeing herself cheered on by an audience of millions of Americans. Or take the ordinary case of a child who receives love and secure attachment from her parents. When she grows up and has her own child, that gift of affirmation and the work that it took to bestow it well become precious to her in a whole new way. Perhaps in times like these, we can glimpse our goodness as drawn from materials we have not provided and as swept up into something greater than something capturable in a single individual's glory. Such moments, although they are perhaps not common enough, do check our sense of our own greatness and power, and make us feel like we are a part of something that transcends us — something *good*.

Of course, many people will not have this feeling, and some will never move beyond it. Nevertheless, such powerful moments can sometimes bring people beyond a fixation on glory as something exclusively their own. To return to the place this chapter began, our best hope is that the Spirit's power uses these moments to make the next step possible. We can give glory's social side its due, too, when we cultivate a culture of grateful dependence and shared goodness, which provides such occasions for God to work. Even when someone doesn't take the next step and acknowledge God as the source of her goodness, living in that kind of community will be a much healthier way to handle glory in the meantime.

When I introduce my students to the concept of vainglory, we do a brainstorming exercise. Who are the most well-known people in America today? It's an easy list to make: in less than a minute we have named celebrities, professional athletes, the fabulously wealthy, the president, and a handful of current rock stars — all household names. Their glory is obvious, but whether they are worthy of attention on a national scale is not. Then I ask my students to make a second list: Who are your personal heroes? This question usually prompts a moment of silence. Heroes? Who has heroes anymore? "Does Batman count?" they ask me with a sheepish laugh. After a few minutes of thinking and scribbling, they hand me their second list. They give me the names of their grandfathers, mothers, high-school coaches, neighborhood mentors, fourth-grade teachers, and youth pastors. The rest of us have never heard of these people. We don't recognize their names. But they are pictures of goodness nonetheless — your pictures and mine. These are the heroes we model our lives after. Although they don't often make the headlines, their goodness shines brightly enough to light the way of those who are inspired by them. Part of our call to be the light of the world and a city on a hill is not only to imitate these people, but also to share their stories and thereby give glory to a different kind of goodness than sensational celebrity. And we can pray that even others who do not have faith yet will see — in our heroes and our imitation of them — a goodness that has both substance and lasting beauty, and therefore a glory that shines for God.

> *Lord, how can man preach thy eternal word?*
> *He is a brittle crazy glass:*
> *Yet in thy Temple thou dost him afford*
> *This glorious and transcendent place,*
> *To be a window, through thy grace.*

> GEORGE HERBERT

Epilogue

Long before any human being saw us,
we are seen by God's loving eyes.

The blessings that we give to each other are expressions
of the blessings that rest on us from all eternity.

Henri J. M. Nouwen, *Life of the Beloved*

VAINGLORY, LIKE ALL of the other capital vices, is a disordered love for something that — if sought in a well-ordered way — is good. To have our goodness recognized and acknowledged is something we long for as human beings. God not only made us good, but in the beginning of everything affirmed our goodness by announcing to the world he had made that we are "very good." *His* acknowledgment came first, and every genuine taste we get on this earth of what it feels like to celebrate that goodness is a reflection of that first word of truth about us.

Pride spoils this view of our goodness and God's affirmation of it. It tempts us to distrust what God said, pronounce it inadequate, and try to produce something better by our own efforts. And so we scramble, breathless, toward greater achievement, or at least the appearance of it, hoping to shore up a track record of goodness that will win us acclaim. Or we hide behind our carefully crafted masks and reputations, worried and defensive about anything that could blow our cover. Our work, our possessions, and our relationships can all become props in the game of trying to win enough approval to feel good about ourselves. The mistake at the root of this unwinnable game is, of course, that approval is not ours to win. We have already been acknowledged. The good words that we really need — "You are known, and you are loved" — have already been spoken from the beginning.

It takes work to live into this true word about ourselves from God, a process Henri Nouwen eloquently describes in *Life of the Beloved.* We are constantly tempted to try to prove ourselves, to show that we are worthy of acceptance and acknowledgment from others. We need all the help we can get to listen well to God's voice. We will need to screen out the fearful lies that come from inside us and the pressures to self-promote that come from outside of us. Others can help by being a community of celebration for us, providing encouragement and affirmation when we can see only a tarnished image of ourselves in the mirror, and reminding us of the bracing truth when we insist on deceiving ourselves that our achievements, polished appearances, and good behavior are sufficient to build a self upon.

There's nothing magical or new about the story of our vainglory. Technology and social media didn't create this problem. Neither did the persecution we received in middle school, the objectification of women, the harsh neglect of our authoritarian parents, economic or racial oppression, and all the rest. While we rightly lament and passionately resist all those broken systems that make the grace we need that much harder to find, this book is not a tirade against our culture, as if fixing our environment would ultimately fix us spiritually. Whatever conditions occasion it, and whatever its external symptoms (or lack of them), vainglory requires self-examination, too. It is, finally, a problem of the heart.

Who am I? What do I need? Where can I find grace, and love, and joy? Do I dare ask for those things, believing that I will receive God's abundant provision, or will I continue trying to supply those things for myself? Our answers are the same old plain truths: we are created good; we are distrustful of God's good word to us and cling madly to our broken selves and systems instead; we are reclaimed and gradually remade into something more glorious than ever before, because through it all we are beloved by a God whose goodness is beyond all fathoming. C. S. Lewis writes that "glory means good report with God, acceptance by God, response, acknowledgment, and welcome into the heart of things."[1] Sometimes it takes an honest look in the mirror — and seeing how much vainglory has colored our view — to realize that freedom comes from giving up the mirrors, the artificial lighting, and the careful poses and instead resting in the knowledge that we are, from the first to the last, beloved in God's sight.

If we live out of that view of ourselves, we will be able to appreciate and celebrate goodness in others without envy or competition. Not only will our own lives show the glorious beauty of living as God's beloved children, but the luminosity of glory will also show through the lives of others. If glory is both our reality and our destiny, then our calling is to acknowledge this in others as much as ourselves. Lewis reminds us that even "the most dull and uninteresting person" we might meet may someday be so glorious we "would be strongly tempted to worship" him or her.[2] Our work to take God's good word about ourselves to heart also helps us to see others' goodness more clearly and appreciate it more fully.

Acknowledging that our glory is already given also frees us from excessive attachment to our own accomplishments or reputation. Whether I succeed or fail, make a big splash or fade into obscurity, my worth is secure, and my offering is a gift to be shared with the world. Detachment from the pressing need to have my achievements be counted publicly is possible when I have a strong sense of being known and loved by God. Then integrity and faithfulness matter more than popularity and public acclaim. At best, that renown is a welcome confirmation; at worst, it is a distraction from the love that I need to keep at the center of everything I do. As Richard Foster puts it, with maturity "we begin to know his Voice" well enough to disentangle it "from the clatter and clamor of human voices."[3] When God's word about the glory of our creation as his beloved children stands behind any goodness we share, then our service, like U2's musical performances, can be enjoyed and offered with freedom and gratitude, without any expectation of worldly glory as its reward.

Nor is worldly scorn its greatest threat. Madeleine L'Engle writes about the source and foundations of true beauty and glory in her poem "People in Glass Houses":

I build my house of shining glass
of crystal
prisms
light, clear,
delicate.

The wind blows
Sets my rooms to singing.
The sun's bright rays
are not held back
but pour
their radiance through the rooms
in sparkles of delight.

And what, you ask, of rain
that leaves blurred muddy streaks
across translucent purity?
What, you ask,
of the throwers of stones?

Glass shatters,
breaks,
sharp fragments pierce my flesh,
darken with blood.
The wind tinkles brittle splinters
of shivered crystal.
The stones crash through.

But never mind.
My house
My lovely shining
fragile broken house
is filled with flowers
and founded on a rock.[4]

Glory is a gift that is shared when we are transparent to God, as in L'Engle's poem, and also when we are transparent to each other. In Victor Hugo's novel *Les Misérables,* a gentle, humble bishop named Bienvenue (meaning "welcome") invites Jean Valjean — a released convict who has been denied shelter everywhere else in town because of his reputation — into his home. He seats Jean at his table by the fire, and they share a meal. In the course of their conversation, the bishop reveals to Jean a truth about

Jean's own goodness that even the man himself, after nineteen years of mistreatment, no longer recognizes or remembers:

> The bishop was sitting next to him and he gently touched his hand. "You didn't have to tell me who you were. This is not my house, it's the house of Jesus Christ. That door does not ask who enters whether he has a name, but whether he has any pain. You are suffering, you are hungry and thirsty; you are welcome. And don't thank me, don't tell me I'm taking you into my home. No one is at home here except the man who is in need of refuge. I'm telling you, who are passing through, you are more at home here than I am myself. Everything here is at your disposal. What do I need to know your name for? Besides, before you told me your name, you had one I knew."
>
> The man opened his eyes in amazement.
>
> "True? You knew what I was called?"
>
> "Yes," replied the bishop. "You are called my brother."[5]

Do we have eyes to see goodness in ourselves and in each other, the "glory and honor" with which God himself crowns us, having created us only a little lower than the heavenly beings (Ps. 8)? That is cause for grateful celebration. "Thus is his Glory Manifest."[6]

Brief Suggestions for Further Reading

On Vainglory and Related Issues

Augustine. *Confessions*. Translated by Henry Chadwick. Oxford: Oxford University Press, 1991.

John Cassian. *The Institutes,* Book XI. Translated by Boniface Ramsey, O.P. Ancient Christian Writers Series, vol. 58. Mahwah, N.J.: Newman Press, 2000.

Desert Fathers. *The Sayings of the Desert Fathers* (VIII: "That Nothing Should Be Done for Show"), in *Western Asceticism,* Library of Christian Classics, vol. 12, edited and translated by Owen Chadwick (Philadelphia: Westminster Press, 1958). Another version of the same text is *The Desert Fathers: Sayings of the Early Christian Monks,* translated and edited by Benedicta Ward (New York: Penguin Classics, 2003).

Rebecca Konyndyk DeYoung. *Glittering Vices: A New Look at the Seven Deadly Sins and Their Remedies.* Grand Rapids: Brazos Press, 2009.

Jennifer A. Herdt. *Putting on Virtue: The Legacy of the Splendid Vices.* Chicago: University of Chicago Press, 2008. This is a scholarly and historical treatment of worries regarding moral formation — e.g., hypocrisy.

C. S. Lewis. "The Weight of Glory." In *The Weight of Glory and Other Addresses.* San Francisco: HarperSanFrancisco, 2001.

Eleonore Stump. *Wandering in Darkness.* Oxford: Oxford University Press, 2010, Part 3, Chapter 12.

On Virtues and Spiritual Disciplines in General

Michael W. Austin and R. Douglas Geivett, editors. *Being Good: Christian Virtues for Everyday Life.* Grand Rapids: Wm. B. Eerdmans, 2012. Andrew Pinsent's chapter on humility discusses forms of pride that are similar to vainglory.

Adele Ahlberg Calhoun. *Spiritual Disciplines Handbook: Practices that Transform Us* (Downers Grove, Ill.: InterVarsity Press, 2005).

Richard J. Foster. *Celebration of Discipline: The Path to Spiritual Growth.* New York: HarperCollins, 1998.

―――. *Freedom of Simplicity: Finding Harmony in a Complex World.* San Francisco: HarperOne, 1973.

Henri Nouwen. *Life of the Beloved. Spiritual Living in a Secular World.* New York: Crossroad, 2002.

⸻. *Making All Things New: An Invitation to the Spiritual Life.* New York: HarperOne, 1981.

Robert C. Roberts. *Spiritual Emotions: A Psychology of Christian Virtues.* Grand Rapids: Wm. B. Eerdmans, 2007.

Notes

Notes to the Introduction

1. See his well-known and classic work of Christian spirituality, *Confessions,* Books II and X especially. Unless otherwise specified, all quotations in the text are from Henry Chadwick's translation (New York: Oxford University Press, 1991).

2. Available in the Archie McFee catalogue online at http://mcphee.com/shop/seven-deadly-sins-wristbands.html.

3. Lady Gaga in an interview with Anderson Cooper, *60 Minutes,* 14 February 2011.

4. Quoted by Jake Halpern, *Fame Junkies: The Hidden Truths behind America's Favorite Addiction* (New York: Houghton Mifflin, 2007), p. 11.

5. Quoted by David Heim, *Christian Century* 104 (3-10 June 1987).

6. Unless indicated otherwise, Scripture references are from the New International Version.

7. N. T. Wright, *Following Jesus: Biblical Reflections on Discipleship* (Grand Rapids: Wm. B. Eerdmans, 1995), p. 84.

8. William Shakespeare, *The Sonnets* (New York: St. Martin's Press, 1980), Sonnet 93.

Notes to Chapter 1

1. This is my translation.

2. For example, answering charges that he is seeking glory for himself, Paul offers this defense and advice: "Let those who boast, boast in the Lord" (2 Cor. 10:17, quoting Jer. 9:24).

3. John Cassian, *The Institutes,* trans. Boniface Ramsey, O.P., Ancient Christian Writers Series, vol. 58 (Mahwah, N.J.: Newman Press, 2000); Book VII; see especially sections VII-IX and XII.

4. *The Sayings of the Fathers,* in *Western Asceticism,* ed. Owen Chadwick, Library of Christian Classics, vol. XII (Philadelphia: Westminster Press, 1958), VI.V, p. 78.

5. Richard Newhauser, *The Early History of Greed: The Sin of Avarice in Early Medieval Thought and Literature* (Cambridge: Cambridge University Press, 2006), chap. 4, pp. 88-91.

6. Evagrius, *Chapters on Prayer,* 12-27, *inter alia,* in *Evagrius of Pontus: The Greek Ascetic Corpus,* trans. Robert E. Sinkewicz, Oxford Early Christian Studies (New York: Oxford University Press, 2003), p. 194. Unless otherwise noted, all quotations from Evagrius's works are from this volume. See also Cassian, *The Institutes,* Book VIII.V-VI.

7. Thomas Aquinas, *Summa theologiae,* trans. Fathers of the English Dominican Province (New York: Benziger Brothers, 1948; reprinted by the Library of Christian Classics, 1981), supplement Q. 42, art. 3, and II-II Q. 151, art. 4. For the complicated and misunderstood reception of this term in church history, see also Cormac Burke's discussion, "A Postscript to the 'Remedium Concupiscentiae,'" *The Thomist* 70 (2006): 481-536.

8. Thomas Aquinas, *On Evil,* trans. Richard Regan (New York: Oxford University

Press, 2003), Q. IX.1, resp. Aquinas explicitly connects glory and "clarity" in this passage, but beauty — implying an attractive display — is also closely related, as I note in footnote 10. Jennifer A. Herdt, in *Putting on Virtue: The Legacy of the Splendid Vices* (Chicago: University of Chicago Press, 2008), offers us an illustration: "Augustine offers examples to inspire imitation, examples that are beautiful, that attract the beholder, that in some way confront the beholder with the beauty of God" (p. 215; see also p. 126). Such cases of goodness have glory that contributes to the edification of others.

9. Anne Lamott, *Operating Instructions* (New York: Anchor Books, 2005), p. 74; see also pp. 34-35.

10. According to Aquinas, beauty is goodness apprehended as pleasing (the love of goodness *as* it appears becoming or fitting to me). Beauty links goodness and its power of attraction via our perception and the affective response it prompts (something like what Aquinas calls *complacentia* or *fruitio* in the appetite). Glory likewise regards others' apprehension (via a display or appearance) of one's goodness and their attraction to it, as it is expressed in attention and public approval (*Summa theologiae* II-II 132.1).

11. Setting aside concerns about God's hiddenness for the moment, I merely want to note that God's goodness *can* in theory be evidenced in every inch of creation.

12. Plato, *Symposium,* trans. A. Nehamas and P. Woodruff (Indianapolis: Hackett, 1997), pp. 55-56.

13. Augustine, *The City of God,* trans. M. Dods (New York: Modern Library, 1993), Book V.14.

14. N. T. Wright, *After You Believe: Why Christian Character Matters* (New York: HarperOne, 2010), p. 131.

15. Aquinas, *Summa theologiae* I-II 132.4 ad 2; see also *Summa theologiae* II-II 103.1 ad 3.

16. The objections are raised in Aquinas, *On Evil* IX.2 obj. 6 and 7.

17. For example, *On Evil* IX.1, resp. Aquinas discusses several passages, noting that the scriptural record is mixed; I will here only mention a prominent and probably familiar instance in the Sermon on the Mount. In other places, the apostle Paul both prohibits boasting and does some boasting "in the Lord" on his own behalf (2 Cor. 10; Jer. 9:23-24).

18. Aquinas, *On Evil* IX.1 ad 1.

19. "Every perfect thing by nature communicates itself to other things as much as it can, and this belongs to everything because everything imitates the first perfect thing, namely, God, who communicates his goodness to everything. And one's goodness is communicated to others regarding both others' existence and others' knowledge. And so it seems to belong to a natural appetite that one wish one's goodness to become known. Therefore, if one relates this desire to a proper end, it will belong to virtue, and if one does not, it will belong to vanity" (Aquinas, *On Evil* IX.1 ad 3).

20. I put the point this way to indicate that one's goodness can be communicated without any intention on the agent's part.

21. Aquinas, *Summa theologiae* II-II 132.1 ad 1.

22. Aquinas, *Summa theologiae* II-II 132.1 ad 3.

23. Aquinas, *Summa theologiae* I-II 132.1 ad 1. In *Summa theologiae* I-II 132.1 ad 3, however, Aquinas importantly qualifies his position on the goodness of glory: "It is

required for human perfection that one should know oneself [and know God]; but not that one should be known by others, wherefore this is not to be desired in itself." This qualification seems to stand in tension with Aquinas's belief that human beings have a natural need to live in community with others. If, as he says in the treatise on law, our sociality is part of our essentially *rational* nature, one would expect being *known* by others to be part of how that sociality is expressed. Why would it not then be required for human perfection that we know others *and* be known by them?

24. It's a testimony to how deep a need it is, I think, that children will seek attention even through negative behavior. Apparently, they value attention so highly from their parents that they behave in such a way as to elicit even negative responses, when the alternative is no response or attention at all.

25. Aquinas's position seems to discount the ways that human beings need acknowledgment and affirmation from others to flourish. Is there an explanation for this? Aquinas does acknowledge that human beings need to be known. His nuanced position is that we do not have a natural desire to be known *as a good sought for its own sake.* "[Glory] may be desired . . . as being *useful* for something." Making ourselves known to others must remain a *bonum utile* — a good which is valuable *only* as directed at something else as its end. It is not immediately clear why he is so insistent on this point; it simply seems excessively stringent. Why think that being known is merely instrumental to community, friendship, and charity?

Aquinas's ultimate reasons may be metaphysical. In this passage on glory, he seems to be less concerned to describe human communities (in this life) than to maintain the sufficiency of our friendship with God (in the next) — our being known and loved by God. Parallel claims in the treatise on happiness about whether friends are required for happiness (*Summa theologiae* I-II 4.8) support this reading. Aquinas claims that human friendships are necessary for the imperfect happiness that is possible in this life, but, strictly speaking, they are not necessary in the next for perfect happiness in union with God. Of course, given the treatise on charity, we can reasonably assume that Aquinas has a picture of the next life that is a rich community of saints in fellowship with one another and with God. So in this passage he must be concerned to make the metaphysical point of God's sufficiency (see *Summa theologiae* I-II 2.8), in tandem with a focus on perfect happiness in the next life.

Does it seem odd in a passage describing potential pitfalls in human relationships (glory-seeking being something we typically do with an audience of others) that Aquinas reminds his readers of a point at which they will technically no longer need human relationships at all? Perhaps not to an audience of Dominicans who have taken vows of renunciation. (This certainly also fits the vocation of the Desert Fathers.) And perhaps this works as an edifying corrective to our tendency to overvalue human glory, even though it is a transitory and temporal good.

26. In the NRSV and the KJV, for example, this connection was also reflected in the marriage relationship (Gen. 4:1: "Adam *knew* Eve his wife . . ."; my emphasis). But Adam's first response to Eve is verbal acknowledgment and affirmation — to her and to God.

27. C. S. Lewis, "The Weight of Glory," in *The Weight of Glory and Other Addresses* (San Franciso: HarperSanFrancisco, 2001), pp. 40-41.

28. Sermonindex, https://twitter.com/sermonindex/statuses/253697505680842752 October 3, 2012.

29. Aristotle, *Nicomachean Ethics,* Bk. VIII.2.4 (1156a).

30. Lewis, "The Weight of Glory," in *The Weight of Glory and Other Addresses,* p. 37.

31. Robin S. Dillon, "A Feminist Concept of Self-Respect," *Hypatia* 7, no. 1 (1992): 54-55.

32. In some respects maintaining a close connection between the agent and her action is appropriate and essential, as we will see in the discussion of habituation in Chapter 4. That's because the process of moral formation aims to forge deep connections between who we are and what we do.

Notes to Chapter 2

1. Bradford Veley, 11 October 2012, www.CartoonStock.com.

2. John Cassian, *The Institutes,* trans. Boniface Ramsey, O.P., Ancient Christian Writers Series, vol. 58 (Mahwah, N.J.: Newman Press, 2000), Book IX.VI.

3. Isaac Watts, "When I Survey the Wondrous Cross," *Psalter Hymnal* (Grand Rapids: CRC Publications, 1987), no. 384.

4. Augustine, *The City of God,* trans. M. Dods (New York: Modern Library, 1993), Book V.14. Augustine's complete case regarding Roman glory occupies chapters 12-20.

5. Augustine, *The City of God,* Book XIV.28.

6. Augustine also makes this point when he argues that justice must include due worship in Book XIX, chapter 21.

7. The connection between the good and the beautiful (or attractive) is evident here again.

8. Cassian, *The Institutes,* Book XII.XIX.

9. John Cassian, *The Conferences,* trans. Boniface Ramsey, O.P., Ancient Christian Writers Series, vol. 57 (Mahwah, N.J.: Newman Press, 1997), Conference V, X.4.

10. Cassian, *The Institutes,* Book XI.VII.

11. Evagrius, *On the Eight Thoughts* 7.10, in *Evagrius of Pontus: The Greek Ascetic Corpus,* trans. Robert E. Sinkewicz, Oxford Early Christian Studies (Oxford: Oxford University Press, 2003).

12. Evagrius, *Praktikos* 30.

13. Cassian, *The Institutes,* Book XI.VII.

14. Halpern recounts Robert Thompson's story on pp. xix-xxiii of *Fame Junkies: The Hidden Truths behind America's Favorite Addiction* (New York: Houghton Mifflin, 2007). This quote is from p. xxii.

15. Halpern, *Fame Junkies,* p. 137.

16. Halpern, *Fame Junkies,* p. 136.

17. Halpern, *Fame Junkies,* p. xxiii.

18. Cassian, *The Institutes,* Book XI.XVI.

19. Homily xiii, *Opus Imperfectum,* quoted in Thomas Aquinas, *Summa theologiae,*

trans. Fathers of the English Dominican Province (New York: Benziger Brothers, 1948; reprinted by the Library of Christian Classics, 1981), II-II 132.3 *sed contra.*

20. Although the list was first written down by Evagrius (as far as historical records show), he inherited and systematized the list already in use among the Christian desert community of monks he joined.

21. Evagrius, *On Thoughts, 1,* in *Evagrius of Pontus.* "Among the demons who set themselves in opposition to the practical life, those ranged first in battle are the ones entrusted with the appetites of gluttony, those who make to us suggestions of avarice, and those who entice us to seek human esteem. All the other demons march along behind these ones and in their turn take up with the people wounded by these. . . . To put it briefly, no one can fall into a demon's power, unless he has first been wounded by those in the front line. For this reason the devil introduced these three thoughts to the Savior: first, he exhorted him to turn stones into bread; then, he promised him the whole world if he would fall down and worship him; and thirdly, he said that if he would listen to him he would be glorified for having suffered no harm from such a fall (Luke 4:1-13). But our Lord showed himself to be above such temptations and commanded the devil to 'get behind him' (cf. Matt. 4:10). Through these things he teaches us too that it is not possible to drive away the devil, unless we have shunned these three thoughts."

22. Why a female monarch? Perhaps for no better reason than that the words naming all the virtues and vices in Latin were feminine nouns.

23. For a clear exposition of four different forms of pride, see Andrew Pinsent, "Humility," in *Being Good: Christian Virtues for Everyday Life,* ed. Michael W. Austin and R. Douglas Geivett (Grand Rapids: Wm. B. Eerdmans, 2012), pp. 250-55. Pinsent's discussion echoes Aquinas's in *On Evil* VIII.4. The original list of four types that Aquinas discusses is from Gregory the Great.

24. There are no offspring associated with pride, because it is the root of the tree, and the seven capital vices themselves count as *its* offspring.

25. Augustine, *Confessions,* trans. Henry Chadwick (Oxford: Oxford University Press, 1991), I.20.

26. In *Augustine of Hippo* (Berkeley and Los Angeles: University of California Press, 1967), pp. 325-26, Peter Brown discusses Augustine's point that "all good things are gifts."

27. The text in which Augustine gives the example of the betrothed is *Tractate 2.11 in Tractates on the First Letter of John.* Paul Griffiths casts this issue in terms of an iconic versus an idolatrous attitude toward created goods in *The Vice of Curiosity: An Essay on Intellectual Appetite* (Winnipeg, Manitoba: Canadian Mennonite University Press, 2006), pp. 40, 66-67, 75-77. Like the woman proposed to in Augustine's example, the prideful person who assumes her goodness is from herself is an inappropriate possessor of a gift from God because she doesn't acknowledge that the goodness is something given to her by another.

Notes to Chapter 3

1. For example, see the British Library's collection of illuminated manuscripts, especially Arundel 44, f. 28v and 29; and Arundel 83, f. 128v, 129: http://www.bl.uk/catalogues/illuminatedmanuscripts/record.asp?MSID=7952&CollID=20&NStart=44 http://www.bl.uk/catalogues/illuminatedmanuscripts/record.asp?MSID=6458&CollID=20&NStart=83.

2. The "trees" representing Aquinas's thought would be rooted in rightly ordered love of God versus disordered love of self. The two ideas are closely related (pride being the ultimate way one's love can be disordered). Rooting each tree in one's ultimate loves also reflects Augustine's influence.

3. Describing the Desert Fathers in *Demons and the Making of the Monk,* David Brakke marks the difference this way: "If vainglory tempts the monk to perform his ascetic labors to win the admiration of others, pride gets the monk to believe his admirers: that he, the monk, really has achieved a great deal. The monk afflicted by pride attributes whatever success he enjoys to himself rather than to the help of God or the angels. Pride fundamentally distorts the monk's relationship with God by preventing the creature from acknowledging his total dependence on the Creator and his grace. . . . Thus one of the symptoms of pride is a breakdown of the monk's relationships with his peers: he despises other people, especially his brothers, as being beneath his level of virtue and knowledge, or he overestimates his importance to other monks . . ." (Cambridge, Mass.: Harvard University Press, 2006), p. 69. Aquinas casts the vices as disordered loves (or desires), so pride is not primarily belief but the excessive or disordered *desire* for this exalted state. We can perhaps best reconcile the two accounts using Robert C. Roberts's view of spiritual emotions as "concern-based construals" — our affective dispositions shape the way we construe the world of our experience (*Spiritual Emotions: A Psychology of Christian Virtues* [Grand Rapids: Wm. B. Eerdmans, 2007], pp. 11-13). In this way, affection and cognition are mutually implicated.

4. Augustine, *Confessions,* trans. Henry Chadwick (Oxford: Oxford University Press, 1991), III.4.

5. Augustine, *Confessions* IV.1.

6. Augustine, *Confessions* IX.4.

7. John Cassian, *The Institutes,* trans. Boniface Ramsey, O.P., Ancient Christian Writers Series, vol. 58 (Mahwah, N.J.: Newman Press, 2000), Book IX.VI.

8. Brakke, *Demons and the Making of the Monk,* p. 68.

9. Cassian, *The Institutes,* Book XI.V.

10. Augustine, *Confessions* X.38.

11. Augustine, *Confessions* II.9.

12. Augustine, *Confessions* II.3.

13. Augustine, *Confessions* IV.14.

14. Augustine, *Confessions* IV.14.

15. Augustine, *Confessions* IV.14.

16. Augustine, *Confessions* IX.1.

17. William Ian Miller, *Faking It* (New York: Cambridge University Press, 2003), p. 8.

18. Quoted in Jake Halpern, *Fame Junkies: The Hidden Truths behind America's Favorite Addiction* (New York: Houghton Mifflin, 2007), p. 72.

Notes to Chapter 4

1. Thomas Aquinas, *Summa theologiae,* trans. Fathers of the English Dominican Province (New York: Benziger Brothers, 1948; reprinted by the Library of Christian Classics, 1981), I-II 84.3-4; Thomas Aquinas, *On Evil,* trans. Richard Regan (New York: Oxford University Press, 2003), VIII.4; Gregory the Great, *Moralia (Morals on the Book of Job),* trans. John Henry Parker (London: J. G. F. and J. Rivington, 1844), 31.xlv.87-91; John Cassian, *The Conferences,* trans. Boniface Ramsey, O.P., Ancient Christian Writers Series, vol. 57 (Mahwah, N.J.: Newman Press, 1997), V.XVI. Gregory does not define what it means to be a capital vice or an offspring of a capital vice, but gives descriptions of the capital vices as both disposing us to and "commanding" other vices.

2. For metaphors of health and disease, cure and symptom, and Christ the physician of souls, see John Cassian, *The Institutes,* trans. Boniface Ramsey, O.P., Ancient Christian Writers Series, vol. 58 (Mahwah, N.J.: Newman Press, 2000), Book XI.XVII, *inter alia.*

3. Discord is opposed to peace, which Aquinas defines as a concord of two (or more) persons' wills. Peace is one of three interior effects of the virtue of *caritas* (love), also located in the will.

4. Peace, an interior effect of the theological virtue of charity, and wrath (an incentive to open conflict) are also relevant to explaining the typical dynamics of a vainglorious disposition. Charity *(caritas)* is the virtue at Aquinas's "root" of the tree of virtues: loving communion with God and neighbor is the foundation for all other virtues. Aquinas writes that the primary effect of love is to unite two people on the basis of likeness of nature. This delight-filled union with another is the basis of a concord of wills, which is peace. Vainglory's last four offspring in particular — obstinacy, discord, contention, and disobedience — are opposed to peace because in cases of potential conflict, deference to others' opinions or wills for the sake of peace seems to reduce our glory. Insofar as glory also appears to us to be a competitive good, diminished by sharing and enhanced by the uniqueness of our claim to it, it can also set us against our neighbor in order to win a round of applause. In this way vainglory can also prompt wrath, since we become angry when our desire for glory is thwarted by one who outdoes us in public conversation or whose command requires that we submit before others and "lose face." We also get angry when we feel injured because that person took away the limelight to which we assumed we had a claim.

5. William Ian Miller, *Faking It* (New York: Cambridge University Press, 2003). Miller distinguishes hypocrisy from several other modes of dissimulation.

6. Miller, *Faking It,* p. 11. This quotation comes from Chapter 2, which is entitled "Hypocrisy and Jesus."

7. Miller, *Faking It,* p. 28.

8. Miller, *Faking It,* p. 28.

9. It is in this sense that shame can function as a preparatory stage in the development of virtue.

10. Augustine, *The City of God,* trans. M. Dods (New York: Modern Library, 1993), V.12.

11. Plato, *Republic,* trans. G. M. A. Grube, rev. C. D. C. Reeve (Indianapolis: Hackett, 1992), Book II, 367d.

12. Miller, *Faking It,* p. 28.

13. For a fuller account of the stages of moral habituation, see M. Burnyeat, "Aristotle on Learning to Be Good," in *Essays on Aristotle's Ethics,* ed. A. O. Rorty (Berkeley and Los Angeles: University of California Press, 1980), pp. 69-92.

14. Aristotle, *Nicomachean Ethics* X.9.

15. Only those who have reached the second stage — i.e., those who have had their passions trained to respond to what is fine and honorable — can be taken on as fitting students of the sort of reflective endorsement of virtuous formation that Aristotle attempts in the *Nicomachean Ethics.* According to Jennifer Herdt, "For Aristotle, this is not the semblance of virtue but simply the ordinary process of moral development" (*Putting on Virtue: The Legacy of the Splendid Vices* [Chicago: University of Chicago Press, 2008], p. 5).

16. This is why Aristotle says that "the feeling of shame is suitable for youth, not for every time of life. For we think it right for young people to be prone to shame, since they live by their feelings, and hence often go astray, but are restrained by shame; and hence we praise young people who are prone to shame" (*Nicomachean Ethics* IV.9 [1128b15-20]).

17. Evagrius, *Praktikos* 58, in *Evagrius of Pontus: The Greek Ascetic Corpus,* trans. Robert E. Sinkewicz, Oxford Early Christian Studies (Oxford: Oxford University Press, 2003), p. 108.

18. With Harry Frankfurt, this situation of potential insincerity might alternately be described in terms of a conflict between first- and second-order desires.

19. This is one worry behind stage-acting that Jane Austen presumes in *Mansfield Park.* Jennifer Herdt, on the other hand, defends cases in which play-acting at being virtuous does help one become virtuous (see *Putting on Virtue,* chap. 5).

20. I do not mean to imply that we ever fully understand ourselves or our motives simply because we can experience our own consciousness in ways that others cannot "from the outside."

21. Miller puts it this way: "The entire psychotherapeutic industry is built on the supposition that other people are often in a much better position to read our inner states than we are, the belief being that even the obscuration wrought on the therapist's vision by his desire for lucre and by his not being inside our heads is not as distorting as the mayhem self-love wreaks on our ability to see ourselves very clearly" (*Faking It,* p. 14).

22. See also extended discussions on this topic in Miller, *Faking It,* and Herdt, *Putting on Virtue.*

23. Herdt describes this as a position inspired primarily by Luther: see *Putting on Virtue,* chap. 6, especially pp. 174, 176-77.

24. N. T. Wright, *After You Believe: Why Christian Character Matters* (New York: HarperOne, 2010), p. 145.

25. On virtue as a developmental concept, see Julia Annas, *Intelligent Virtue* (New York: Oxford University Press, 2011). See, for example, p. 14.

26. Aristotle, *Nicomachean Ethics* III.5 (1114b10).

27. Gregg A. Ten Elshof, *I Told Me So: Self-Deception and the Christian Life* (Grand Rapids: Wm. B. Eerdmans, 2009), pp. 133-34.

28. Ten Elshof, *I Told Me So,* p. 133.

29. Herdt also makes this point in *Putting on Virtue,* p. 82.

30. Søren Kierkegaard, *Works of Love,* in *The Essential Kierkegaard,* ed. and trans. Howard V. Hong and Edna H. Hong (Princeton: Princeton University Press, 1980), IX.201-215.

31. In most contemporary moral theories, duties and obligations are both relatively contextless and yet still morally compulsory; neither does producing the best outcome seem to be conditioned by one's moral character. Moreover, contemporary ethical theories that focus on duties or consequences tend toward what I'll call a "snapshot" view of the moral life, rather than a gradual, long-term, developmental one. For a fuller discussion of the difference it makes whether one is a learner or an expert, see Annas, *Intelligent Virtue,* pp. 41-44.

32. See Herdt, *Putting on Virtue,* for a fuller explanation of why this cooperation is itself grace-enabled, not a prideful or Pelagian assertion of human agency. Herdt also effectively argues that cooperation is essential, rather than advocating total passivity on our part (pp. 340-52).

33. Following Lee Yearley, Herdt distinguishes between counterfeits of virtue and semblances of virtue; only in the former cases is there intention to deceive about one's good character (*Putting on Virtue,* p. 4). Aquinas uses the term "simulacra" to name vices that imitate virtues (e.g., see *Summa theologiae* II-II 55).

34. Aquinas, *Summa theologiae* II-II 109.

35. To paraphrase Aquinas, truthfulness is like justice in that it is other-directed and has something of the notion of due, but it falls short of obligations to verbally accurate truth-telling that come under the notion of justice, strictly speaking (e.g., promises and other contractual oral commitments, witnessing in court, the avoidance of libel and slander), which Aquinas calls "legal due." As such he designates truthfulness a "potential part" of justice (*Summa theologiae* II-II 109.3 and ad 3): "Now the virtue of truthfulness has two things in common with justice. In the first place it is directed to another, since the manifestation, which we have stated to be an act of truth, is directed to another, inasmuch as one person manifests to another the things that concern himself. In the second place, justice sets up a certain equality between things, and this the virtue of truthfulness does also, for it equals signs to the things which concern a person. Nevertheless, the virtue of truthfulness falls short of the proper aspect of justice, as to the notion of debt: for this virtue does not regard legal debt, which justice considers, but rather the moral debt, insofar as out of equity, one person owes another a manifestation of the truth. Therefore truth is a part of justice, being annexed thereto as a secondary virtue to its principal."

36. Aquinas, *Summa theologiae* II-II 109.3 ad 3.

37. I take the term from Charles Taylor, *Sources of the Self: The Making of the Modern*

Identity (Cambridge: Cambridge University Press, 1989) and *The Ethics of Authenticity* (Cambridge, Mass.: Harvard University Press, 1992).

38. Ordinary cases of lying are opposed to cases of lying in contexts where truth-telling is legally obligatory — i.e., in court (see note 35).

39. Aquinas, *Summa theologiae* II-II 111.

40. Josef Pieper, *The Four Cardinal Virtues,* trans. Clara Winston et al. (Notre Dame: University of Notre Dame Press, 1966), p. 15.

41. Tim Rohan, "Sandusky Gets 30 Years for Sexual Abuse," *The New York Times,* 9 October 2012.

42. Gregory, *Moralia* 31.xiii.24, quoted in Aquinas, *Summa theologiae* II-II 111.2 ad 1.

43. Pieper, *The Four Cardinal Virtues,* p. 21.

Notes to Chapter 5

1. Thomas Aquinas, *On Evil,* trans. Richard Regan (New York: Oxford University Press, 2003), IX.1, resp.

2. Aristotle, *Nicomachean Ethics* IV.3 1124a1-5.

3. There are five objections instead of the standard three, and three vices opposed by way of excess instead of the standard one. The discussion is also long enough to strain the summary nature of the *Summa theologiae,* where Aquinas's discussion takes place. (See *Summa theologiae,* trans. Fathers of the English Dominican Province [New York: Benziger Brothers, 1948; reprinted by the Library of Christian Classics, 1981].) One other note: Pusillanimity is the single vice of deficiency opposed to magnanimity. Those with pusillanimity characteristically underestimate their capacities and shrink back from attempting great acts in order to avoid the possibility of thereby publicly exposing their shortcomings or failures. The pusillanimous fear not only their failures but also the shame generated by others' observation of their failures. Hence pusilla-nimity's opposition to magnanimity, which is concerned not only with great acts but also with great honors.

4. The whole passage reads as follows: "First, we must not allow ourselves to do anything at the behest of vanity or for the sake of acquiring empty glory. Then we must attempt to maintain by a consistent observance those things that we have begun well, lest the disease of vainglory steal in later on and bring to naught all the fruit of our labors. Too, we must strive utterly to reject as the stuff of boastfulness whatever is not generally accepted and practiced as part of the way of life of the brothers, and we must also avoid those things that could set us apart from others and that would gain us praise from human beings, as if we were the only ones who could do them" (John Cassian, *The Institutes,* trans. Boniface Ramsey, O.P., Ancient Christian Writers Series, vol. 58 [Mahwah, N.J.: Newman Press, 2000], Book XI.XVIII).

5. See Aquinas's summary of Benedict's twelve steps (from chap. 7 of the *Rule*), in contrast with Aristotle's description of the magnanimous man (*Summa theologiae* II-II 161.6).

6. Humility is the root of the tree of virtues (charity is the "root and mother" of

Thomistic virtues; see Aquinas, *Summa theologiae* II-II 23.8 ad 2 and ad 3). St. Benedict outlined the twelve steps of humility in his *Rule,* chap. 7.

7. See 2 Peter 1:3-11 and Aquinas, *Summa theologiae* II-II 129.3. For a more thorough discussion of magnanimity's status as a Christian virtue, see David A. Horner, "What It Takes to Be Great: Aristotle and Aquinas on Magnanimity," *Faith and Philosophy* 15, no. 4 (October 1998): 415-44; Rebecca Konyndyk DeYoung, "Aquinas's Virtues of Acknowledged Dependence: A New Measure of Greatness," *Faith and Philosophy* 21, no. 2 (April 2004): 214-27; Andrew Pinsent, *The Second-Person Perspective in Aquinas's Ethics* (New York: Routledge, 2012), pp. 77-83; and Jennifer A. Herdt, *Putting on Virtue: The Legacy of the Splendid Vices* (Chicago: University of Chicago Press, 2008), pp. 38-43, 77-80. I reject Pinsent's analysis of Hitler as an example of magnanimous acknowledged dependence on my definition of the virtue because a quest for world domination and racial purity (never mind one accomplished through genocide) is not an act conducive to any good end, or one consonant with human flourishing. But this condition must be met for an act dependent on divine aid to count as an act of virtue at all. We simply need Aristotle's familiar distinction between real and apparent goods to show that while Hitler *thinks* of his end as a human good (for the great attainment of which he is dependent on divine aid), it is in fact a perversion of it. Like Philippa Foot's "courageous" criminal, the Hitler case is at best a case of virtue's dispositional simulacrum, not the real thing. (See Philippa Foot, *Virtues and Vices* [Oxford: Oxford University Press, 1978], p. 15.)

8. After the Annunciation, Mary is likely shunned and shamed by her community when her pregnancy is discovered; she nevertheless sings of the Lord's regard for her lowly estate. But human opinion is not entirely lacking: she sees herself as blessed because her obedience will be a blessing to future generations who will recognize her son as the savior, and she has the comfort of Elizabeth's affirmation in the present. I think it is telling that God does not leave her without human affirmation; rather, he provides it as a confirmation and an encouragement to remain faithful to his own word about her.

9. Eleonore Stump, *Wandering in Darkness: Narrative and the Problem of Suffering* (New York: Oxford University Press, 2010), p. 362.

10. Aquinas, *Summa theologiae* II-II 55.4.

11. Here is the rest of the quotation: ". . . and magnanimity makes him despise others insofar as they fall away from God's gifts: since he does not think so much of others as to do anything wrong for their sake. Yet humility makes us honor others and esteem them better than ourselves, insofar as we see some of God's gifts in them . . ." (Aquinas, *Summa theologiae* I-II 129.3 ad 4).

12. To put the text in its medieval context: the great acts of virtue that Aquinas was thinking of here include primarily the counsels of perfection — the three religious vows of poverty, chastity, and obedience.

13. Presumption here is different from the vice of pride. See Aquinas's own explanation of the difference between these in *Summa theologiae* II-II 162.8 ad 3 and II-II 130; *On Evil* VIII.4. To put it simply, pride and humility seem to be principally concerned with one's *position* or *status* (one of superiority to another or subjection to another), while

presumption, magnanimity, and pusillanimity are principally concerned with one's *power to act,* and the actions and passions that prompt and are prompted by excessive or deficient estimations of our own power. See *Summa theologiae* II-II 161.1 ad 3 and 162.1 ad 3 for Aquinas's explanations on this subject.

14. This English translation can be misleading. Aquinas is working from the Vulgate's translation of 1 Cor. 13:5: "rude" in English is *ambitiosa* in Latin and ασχημονει in the Greek, meaning "to behave in an unseemly manner, to act indecorously"; such shamefulness is the opposite of honor. Aquinas takes "ambition" in a technical sense to mean the excessive desire for honor (and the unbecoming use of such). See *Summa theologiae* II-II 131.1-2.

15. The great acts of virtue are magnanimity's end, while honor is its object or matter. I am leaving many such complications aside in this chapter.

16. Aquinas, *Summa theologiae* II-II 132.2.

17. Here the link with magnanimity makes vainglory sound like it applies more in political and ecclesiastical affairs than within the confines of the monastery.

18. In the case of the vices opposed to magnanimity, these acts can either be truly great, or be taken to be great in the eyes of others, or be taken to be great in one's own judgment (mistaken or not).

19. Interview in March 2011, first published in *Time* magazine, August 25, 2014, p. 60.

20. Robert C. Roberts and W. Jay Wood, *Intellectual Virtues* (Oxford: Clarendon Press, 2007), pp. 241, 255.

21. Roberts and Wood, *Intellectual Virtues,* p. 238.

22. Mihalyi Csikszentmihalyi, quoted in Julia Annas, *Intelligent Virtue* (New York: Oxford University Press, 2011), pp. 70-72.

Notes to Chapter 6

1. John Cassian, *The Institutes,* trans. Boniface Ramsey, O.P., Ancient Christian Writers Series, vol. 58 (Mahwah, N.J.: Newman Press, 2000), Book XI.XVII.

2. *The Sayings of the Fathers,* in *Western Asceticism,* ed. Owen Chadwick, Library of Christian Classics, vol. XII (Philadelphia: Westminster Press, 1958), VIII.10, p. 99 ("That nothing should be done for show").

3. *The Sayings of the Desert Fathers: The Alphabetic Collection,* trans. Benedicta Ward (Trappist, Ky.: Cistercian Publications, 1974; revised edition, 1984), p. 132.

4. Here I note Julia Annas's point that the exercise of virtue, when one becomes proficient in it, tends to be self-effacing, both regarding the virtue being exercised and the person exercising it. But spiritual direction and self-examination, as practices of reflecting on the self and its exercise of virtue (or vice), both seem to preclude such effacement. See *Intelligent Virtue* (New York: Oxford University Press, 2011), pp. 72, 162.

5. Cassian, *The Institutes,* Book XI.XIX.

6. Cassian, *The Institutes,* Book XI.XIX.

7. But like Abba Moses's self-denigration, does it edge perilously close to the vices of deception we looked at in Chapter 4? One might raise worries about pretending to

be less pious than one actually is as itself an expression of piety (or humility). Is this a recommendation of intentional deception or merely concealment? Benedict could probably reply that lowering oneself is a discipline and a practice; like other practices, one has to behave in certain ways in order to form one's mind and heart rightly in accord with that behavior, a process of integration which takes time (Aquinas, *Summa theologiae*, trans. Fathers of the English Dominican Province [New York: Benziger Brothers, 1948; reprinted by the Library of Christian Classics, 1981], II-II 161, 1, ad 2): in addition to the "gift of grace," we "arrive at humility . . . by human effort, whereby one first restrains the outward man, and afterwards succeeds in plucking out the inward root." Aquinas notes, when discussing Benedict's steps of humility, that there is always something to honor in another (namely, the image of Christ) that is better than something in you (your own sinful nature), and by making that comparison, one can *truthfully* lower oneself vis-à-vis another in any circumstance (see *Summa theologiae* II-II 103, 2 ad 3, and 161, 1 ad 1).

8. Augustine, *Confessions*, trans. Henry Chadwick (Oxford: Oxford University Press, 1991), X.37.

9. Evagrius, *Thoughts* 15, in *Evagrius of Pontus: The Greek Ascetic Corpus*, trans. Robert E. Sinkewicz, Oxford Early Christian Studies (New York: Oxford University Press, 2003), p. 194.

10. Boethius, *The Consolation of Philosophy*, Book III.iv, trans. Richard H. Green (New York: Macmillan/Library of Liberal Arts, 1962).

11. Here Gregory the Great's point that vainglory and envy (including its offspring vice, *Schadenfreude*) are closely related vices is certainly vindicated. This is a point I'll return to in Chapter Seven.

12. Jake Halpern, *Fame Junkies: The Hidden Truths behind America's Favorite Addiction* (New York: Houghton Mifflin, 2007), p. 112.

13. Evagrius, *Eulogios* 14, in *Evagrius of Pontus*.

14. Dietrich Bonhoeffer, *Life Together* (San Francisco: HarperOne, 2009), p. 80.

15. Josef Pieper, *The Four Cardinal Virtues*, trans. Clara Winston et al. (Notre Dame: University of Notre Dame Press, 1966), p. 20.

16. Richard J. Foster, *Freedom of Simplicity: Finding Harmony in a Complex World* (San Francisco: HarperOne, 1973), p. 68.

17. *The Sayings of the Desert Fathers*, IV.7: "They said of Abba Agatho that for three years he kept a pebble in his mouth, to teach himself silence."

18. Adele Ahlberg Calhoun, *Spiritual Disciplines Handbook: Practices That Transform Us* (Downers Grove, Ill.: InterVarsity Press, 2005), pp. 108-9.

19. Foster, *Freedom of Simplicity*, p. 107.

20. Foster, *Freedom of Simplicity*, pp. 114, 116.

21. Foster, *Freedom of Simplicity*, p. 108.

22. Foster, *Freedom of Simplicity*, p. 93.

23. "On Quiet," no. 16, in *The Desert Fathers: Sayings of the Early Christian Monks*, trans. and ed. by Benedicta Ward (New York: Penguin Classics, 2003), p. 11.

24. Henri Nouwen, *Making All Things New: An Invitation to the Spiritual Life* (New York: HarperOne, 1981), pp. 69-80.

25. Calhoun, *The Spiritual Disciplines Handbook*, p. 110.

26. Calhoun, *The Spiritual Disciplines Handbook,* pp. 112-13.

27. Calhoun, *The Spiritual Disciplines Handbook,* p. 113.

28. Foster, *Freedom of Simplicity,* p. 107.

29. Bonhoeffer, *Life Together,* p. 111.

30. Robin Dillon, "Toward a Feminist Conception of Self-Respect," *Hypatia* 7, no. 1 (1992): 61.

31. Augustine, Sermon 339:1-4, in *The Works of Saint Augustine: A Translation for the 21st Century,* Part III, vol. 9, trans. Edmund Hill (Hyde Park, N.Y.: New City Press, 1994), p. 279. Thank you to William Harmless for bringing this passage to my attention.

32. Augustine, Sermon 339:1-4, in *The Works of Saint Augustine,* Part III, vol. 9, p. 279.

33. Augustine, Sermon 339:1-4, in *The Works of Saint Augustine,* Part III, vol. 9, p. 279.

34. *The Sayings of the Desert Fathers: The Alphabetic Collection,* Iota #7, p. 103.

Notes to Chapter 7

1. Servais Pinckaers, *The Sources of Christian Ethics,* trans. Sr. Mary Thomas Noble, O.P. (Washington, D.C.: Catholic University of America Press, 1995), is a notable example: he notes the omission of a discussion of beatitude, the Holy Spirit, and grace and the focus on obligation, law, and conscience (pp. 254-79).

2. On this latter point, his system of virtues is perennially controversial because he asserts that true and perfect virtues are infused by the Holy Spirit and not through our own effort or practice. He therefore has to defend his conceptualization of them as *human habits,* despite his strong view of their divine causes.

3. Thomas Aquinas, *Summa theologiae,* trans. Fathers of the English Dominican Province (New York: Benziger Brothers, 1948; reprinted by the Library of Christian Classics, 1981), III, prologue.

4. Evagrius, *Eulogios* 14, in *Evagrius of Pontus: The Greek Ascetic Corpus,* trans. Robert E. Sinkewicz, Oxford Early Christian Studies (New York: Oxford University Press, 2003).

5. Cassian, *The Institutes,* trans. Boniface Ramsey, O.P., Ancient Christian Writers Series, vol. 58 (Mahwah, N.J.: Newman Press, 2000), XII.IX-X.

6. The Book of Wisdom, which lists the four cardinal virtues (prudence, justice, courage, and temperance) in Chapter 8, is taken to be less authoritative by most Protestants than 1 Corinthians 13, with its list of the three theological virtues (faith, hope, and love). Interestingly, however, the Protestant tradition tends not to emphasize the three theological virtues *as virtues,* perhaps because this term is imported from a Greek philosophical tradition that was pre-Christian — although there are good reasons to think that is, by itself, not an adequate rationale. The lack of virtue talk in Protestantism now likely reflects larger historical shifts in ethical preoccupations with the law and commandments in the fourteenth century and following.

7. N. T. Wright, *After You Believe: Why Christian Character Matters* (New York: HarperOne, 2010), chapter 5.3, esp. pp. 157-58.

8. I am setting aside philosophical complications about shared moral responsibility here.

9. Josef Pieper, *The Four Cardinal Virtues,* trans. Clara Winston et al. (Notre Dame: University of Notre Dame Press, 1966), chap. 1, sec. 2 (pp. 10-22).

10. Gregory the Great, *Moralia (Morals on the Book of Job),* trans. John Henry Parker (London: J. G. F. and J. Rivington, 1844), XXXI.xvl.89.

11. Charles Taylor, *The Ethics of Authenticity* (Cambridge, Mass.: Harvard University Press, 1992), p. 29.

12. Gabriele Taylor makes a fascinating and psychologically astute attempt to explain the self-destructive and self-defeating character of the vices in purely naturalistic terms in *Deadly Vices* (New York: Oxford University Press, 2006). Although she does not work with an objective notion of the human good, she seems to assume that human agency is necessary for it. She does not, however, address the original designation or character of the vices as *capital* or source vices, nor does she treat them under the overtly theological designation of *sinful* habits.

13. The Christian view of our ultimate end as a love relationship with God (and the glory that communion brings us) also makes clear that eternal goodness is not exclusive to an individual, but is a shareable good redounding to the good of all. This is also a key premise of Christian practices of celebration, which rejoice in gifts as benefiting the whole community rather than exalting the excellence of one member in a way that lessens or comes at the expense of others. The flip side of thinking of vainglory as a social vice is thinking of the Christian life as relational and its virtues as gifts to a community that's itself essential to our individual flourishing.

14. The other part may be vainglory's historical conflation with pride. It's interesting that pride is not a vice that is often taken seriously by a secular culture, either. Today the term is used as positively as it is pejoratively. See, for example, Michael Eric Dyson, *Pride: The Seven Deadly Sins* (New York: Oxford University Press, 2006). For an excellent contemporary account of pride as a vice, see Robert C. Roberts, "The Vice of Pride," *Faith and Philosophy* 26, no. 2 (2009): 119-33.

Notes to Epilogue

1. C. S. Lewis, "The Weight of Glory," in *The Weight of Glory and Other Addresses* (San Francisco: HarperSanFrancisco, 2001), pp. 40-41.

2. Lewis, "The Weight of Glory," p. 42.

3. Richard J. Foster, *Freedom of Simplicity: Finding Harmony in a Complex World* (San Francisco: HarperOne, 1973), p. 109.

4. Madeleine L'Engle, "People in Glass Houses," in *The Ordering of Love* (Colorado Springs: Waterbrook Press, 2005), pp. 23-24.

5. Victor Hugo, *Les Misérables,* trans. Julie Rose (New York: Random House, 2008), p. 73.

6. Madeleine L'Engle, "Epiphany," in *The Ordering of Love,* p. 139.

Index

Acknowledgment, 6, 21, 22, 29, 44, 45, 49, 51, 59, 100-101, 101-2

Adam and Eve, 35, 37

Advertising, 44; and presumption of novelties, 38, 39, 57

Affirmation, 20-21, 22, 23, 24, 25, 51, 58, 59, 100-101, 101-2, 138n25; as Adam's first response to Eve, 138n26; and the behavior of children, 20, 138n24; Elizabeth's affirmation of Mary, 146n8; Jesus' affirmation of the woman who anoints his feet, 78-79

After You Believe: Why Christian Character Matters (Wright), 66-67

Ambition, 80, 82-83

Anger. *See* Wrath

Annas, Julia, 144n25, 144n31, 147n4

Anthony, Saint, 77

Appearance, 4-6, 9, 27, 44, 48, 51

Applause, 1, 15, 25, 29, 42, 45, 50, 85, 123; addiction to, 8; silently applauding oneself, 47

Approval, 6, 14, 23, 31, 43, 44, 45, 48, 49, 50, 51, 55; conditional approval, 24

Aquinas, Thomas, 4, 7, 31, 32, 53, 62, 87, 92, 108, 111, 113, 122, 137n8, 137nn16-17, 137n19, 140n23, 145n3; on ambition, 147n14; on beauty, 137n8, 137n10; on Benedict's steps of humility, 148n7; on the distinction between pride and vainglory, 42-43; on glory, 14, 15, 17, 18-19, 20, 26, 104, 137n10, 137-38n23; on human community, 22;

on human relationships, 138n25; on hypocrisy, 72; on love, 142n4; on magnanimity, 75-83, 92, 146n11; on peace, 142n3; on "simulacra," 144n33; on truthfulness, 56, 69, 70, 71-72, 144n35; on vainglory, 35, 73; on vainglory's offspring vices, 57, 58; on vices, 36, 38, 76, 82, 109-10, 141n3; on virtues, 82, 110, 149n2; on wrath, 13

Aristotle, 22, 43, 61; distinction between real and apparent goods, 146n7; on friendship, 22; on the "great-souled man," 43, 76, 77-78, 145n5; on shame, 143n16; on the stages of moral formation, 63-65, 143n15

Attachment studies in psychology, 101

Attention, 15, 17, 18-19, 20-21, 25, 33, 43, 44, 45, 48, 49, 51, 55; avoidance of, 88-92; and the behavior of children, 20-21; obsession with, 32-33

Attentiveness, 21, 22, 119

Attraction, 15

Audience, 33, 35, 50; creating an audience in one's own head, 34-35, 74, 98; intended audience, 25, 28; lack of in the spiritual discipline of solitude, 97-98

Augustine, 2, 7, 11-12, 39, 40, 42, 62, 77, 92, 110, 124, 125, 136n1, 139n6, 140n27; on glory, 19; late-life sermon of, 8, 102-4, 119; life story of, 8, 41, 44-45, 47, 48-51, 52;